Radical Visions
of the Future

Studies of the Research Institute on
International Change, Columbia University
Zbigniew Brzezinski, series editor

Zbigniew Brzezinski is Herbert Lehman Professor of Government and director of the Research Institute on International Change at Columbia University, where he has taught since 1960. Dr. Brzezinski serves also in the Carter administration as assistant to the president for national security affairs.

Radicalism in the Contemporary Age
Seweryn Bialer and Sophia Sluzar, editors
Vol. 2 — Radical Visions of the Future

To understand contemporary society, it has become more
and more essential to understand the phenomenon of radicalism—the aspirations of radical movements, the strategies and
tactics of radicalism, and the impact of radicalism on contemporary society. *Radicalism in the Contemporary Age*
grew out of the recognition of this need. A study in three
volumes, it is based on original papers that were prepared for
a series of workshops held in 1975 at the Research Institute
on International Change, Columbia University, and then
revised in light of the workshop discussions.

This volume, *Radical Visions of the Future,* treats the
visionary component of radicalism—the component that
encompasses the image of the good society and that provides
inspiration and possibly direction to a radical movement in
its rejection of the existing order. The study inquires whether
and how the visionary aspect in contemporary radical movements differs from that in earlier ones. In the introductory
chapter, Leszek Kolakowski deals with the nature and moti-
vation of utopian thought. Robert Nisbet's essay provides a
historic overview of utopian literature as a secularized response to such specific developments as industrialization.
Bertell Ollman attempts a reconstruction of the "good
society" as envisaged by Marx. Maurice Meisner examines the
tension between the utopian and dystopian elements in Mao's
thought, and Dick Howard portrays the mood and the perceptions of the New Left. The closing essay, by Marcus
Raskin, represents a critique of contemporary futurological
planning in Western democracies.

Sources of Contemporary Radicalism, the first volume

of this study, includes contributions on the definitional aspects and the sources and carriers of contemporary radicalism, the lack of socialism in the United States, the phenomenon of student radicalism in the U.S., differing radical responses in France and Italy after World War II, and peasant discontent in modern times. The closing chapter is a valuable interpretative survey of the literature on radicalism.

The third volume, *Strategies and Impact of Contemporary Radicalism,* deals principally with three themes: the models and strategies of revolutionary change adopted by diverse radical movements, the impact of radicalism on the societies where it exists, and the prospects of radical success in the political arena.

* * *

Seweryn Bialer, an expert on comparative communism and revolutionary change, teaches in the Department of Political Science at Columbia University and is director of programs at the Research Institute on International Change.

Sophia Sluzar is assistant director of the Research Institute on International Change. A doctoral candidate in Columbia University's Department of History, she has taught modern European history at Pace College for four years.

Radicalism
in the
Contemporary Age

Seweryn Bialer, editor
Sophia Sluzar, associate editor

Volume 2

Radical Visions
of the Future

CONTRIBUTORS

DICK HOWARD   LESZEK KOLAKOWSKI
MAURICE MEISNER   ROBERT NISBET
BERTELL OLLMAN   MARCUS RASKIN

PREFACE BY ZBIGNIEW BRZEZINSKI

WESTVIEW PRESS
BOULDER COLORADO

A Westview Special Study

Copyright © 1977 by the Research Institute on International Change, Columbia University

Published in 1977 in the United States of America by
Westview Press, Inc.
1898 Flatiron Court
Boulder, Colorado 80301
Frederick A. Praeger, Publisher and Editorial Director

Library of Congress Cataloging in Publication Data

Main entry under title:

Radical visions of the future.

(Radicalism in the contemporary age; v. 2)
(Studies of the Research Institute on International Change, Columbia University)
    Papers from a series of workshops held at the Research Institute on International Change, Columbia University, Feb.–May 1975.
    1. Communism—1945-   —Congresses.
2. Radicalism—Congresses. 3. Prediction—Congresses. I. Kolakowski, Leszek. II. Series. III. Series: Columbia University. Research Institute on International Change. Studies of the Research Institute on International Change, Columbia University.
HX15.R25 vol. 2 [HX13.A3]   320.5'3s [320.5'3]
ISBN 0-89158-131-6   76-52453

Printed and bound in the United States of America

Contents

Preface

The three volumes composing *Radicalism in the Contemporary Age* are the outcome of a series of workshops held at the Research Institute on International Change between February and May 1975. Four workshops were organized to examine the sources of radicalism; the aspirations of radical movements; the strategies and tactics of radicalism; and the conditions of success and the impact of radicalism on contemporary societies.

The first workshop was designed to explore whether and to what extent the explanations given in past studies for the development of radicalism—explanations such as rapid changes in the stratification system, rising expectations, the characteristics of marginality in individuals, and so forth—still held true. It seemed possible that contemporary conditions required a different explanatory framework for radical behavior. The second workshop, dealing with the aspirations of radical movements, was organized because it seemed important to examine not only the much neglected "visionary" aspect of radical movements, but also the function of this vision in the formation, development, or decline of radical movements. By developing and linking new revolutionary theories with new forms of revolutionary warfare—for example, in the perception of the relation of forces underlying the revolutionary process, in the selection of methods, and in the expectations of success—radical movements since World War II have demonstrated distinctive characteristics.

Thus, the third workshop was devoted to a partial examination of these aspects of radicalism. The final workshop dealt not only with questions regarding the kinds of revolutions possible in the contemporary world, but also with conditions of stability in industrialized democracies in an era of rapid global change. It should be noted that the focus of the workshops was on radicalism in the United States and Western Europe; developing and communist societies entered only marginally into the discussions.

We attempted to assure continuity in the workshops by inviting to all four a core group of the same participants. We also tried to assure that the participants would be heterogeneous in terms of age as well as in their political and methodological orientations. The papers for the workshops were distributed to the participants in advance so that each session would be devoted entirely to discussion led off by a principal commentator.

It had been our original intention to publish not only the papers from each workshop, but also the remarks of the principal commentators as well as the discussions. The constraints of publication have necessitated the abandonment of this ambitious scheme and, we regret, the elimination of some papers. Nevertheless, complete transcripts of the discussions and the original papers, as well as summaries, are available and can be consulted at the institute's library.

An enterprise of this nature involves the efforts of many persons. First of all, I would like to thank the principal commentators and the authors of the papers for the workshops. Seymour Martin Lipset (then at Harvard University, now at Stanford University) spoke at the first workshop, Februrary 5, 1975, on "Sources of Radicalism in the United States"; Juan Linz (Yale University) wrote a paper on "The Sources of Radicalism in the Iberian Peninsula"; and Sidney Tarrow (Cornell University) wrote on "Sources of French Radicalism: Archaic Protest, Antibureaucratic Rebellion, and Anticapitalist Revolt." The principal commentator was Mark Kesselman (Columbia University). The paper by Stanley

Rothman (Smith College) et al., "Ethnic Variations in Student Radicalism: Some New Perspectives," was discussed by Dr. David Gutmann (Center of Psycho-Social Studies, Chicago). The principal commentator for Henry Landsberger's (University of North Carolina at Chapel Hill) paper, "The Sources of Rural Radicalism," was Donald Zagoria (Hunter College, City University of New York). William H. Overholt (Hudson Institute) contributed a paper on "Sources of Radicalism and Revolution: A Survey of Literature."

At the workshop on March 5, the discussion of a paper by Robert Nisbet (Columbia University), "The Function of the Vision of the Future in Radical Movements," was initiated by Leszek Kolakowski (Oxford University). William Griffith (Massachusetts Institute of Technology) and Ira Katznelson (University of Chicago) discussed papers by Bertell Ollman (New York University), "Marx's Vision of Communism: A Reconstruction"; Maurice Meisner (University of Wisconsin), "Utopian and Dystopian Elements in the Maoist Vision of the Future"; and Dick Howard (State University of New York, Stony Brook), "The Future as Present: Political and Theoretical Implications." Marcus Raskin (Institute of Policy Studies) spoke on "Futurology and Its Radical Critique."

At the April 2 workshop the principal commentator on Alexander Dallin's (Stanford University) paper, "Retreat from Optimism: On Marxian Models of Revolution," was Michel Oksenberg (University of Michigan). Bogdan Denitch (Queens College, City University of New York) introduced the discussion of Henry Bienen's (Princeton University) paper, "New Theories of Revolution," and Sidney Tarrow led off the discussion on Peter Lange's (Harvard University) paper, "The French and Italian Communist Parties: Postwar Strategy and Domestic Society." Klaus Mehnert (*Osteuropa*) gave the initial comments on Massimo Teodori's (Rome) paper, "The New Lefts in Europe."

At the fourth workshop the discussions were initiated by Lewis Coser (State University of New York, Stony Brook), on John Dunn's (Cambridge University) "The Success and

Failure of Modern Revolutions"; Douglas Chalmers (Columbia University), on Alfred Stepan's (Yale University) "Inclusionary and Exclusionary Military Responses to Radicalism with Special Attention to Peru"; and Seweryn Bialer (Columbia University), on Charles Maier's (Harvard University, now at Duke University) "Beyond Revolution? Resistance and Vulnerability to Radicalism in Advanced Western Societies." Samuel Huntington (Harvard University) spoke on "The Meanings of Stability in the Modern Era."

In addition to the authors of papers and the principal commentators, the participants in the discussions at the workshops were Isaac Balbus (York, City University of New York), Thomas Bernstein (Yale University, now at Columbia University), Bernard Brown (Graduate Center, City University of New York), Mauro Calamandrei (*L'Espresso*), Alexander Erlich (Columbia University), Stuart Fagan (Columbia University), Oleh Fedyshyn (Richmond, City University of New York), Clifford Geertz (Institute for Advanced Study, Princeton University), Charles Issawi (Columbia University, now at Princeton University), Joachim Kondziela (University of Lublin, Poland), Irving Kristol (Graduate Center, City University of New York, and *Public Interest*), Robbin Laird (Columbia University), Robert Lane (Yale University), S. Robert Lichter (Harvard University), Egon Neuberger (State University of New York, Stony Brook), William Odom (U.S. Military Academy, West Point), Harvey Picker (Columbia University), Carl Riskin (Columbia University), Joseph Rothschild (Columbia University), James Schmidt (Columbia University, now at University of Texas), Bhabani Sen Gupta (Nehru University, New Delhi), Allan Silver (Columbia University), Bruce Smith (Columbia University), Fritz Stern (Columbia University), and Ronald Tiersky (Amherst College).

It gives me pleasure to acknowledge the important contribution rendered by the staff of the institute. Mitchell Brody was helpful in the early planning stages of the workshops. Richard Royal helped not only with the organizational aspects but also in the preparation of summaries of the discussions. Richard Snyder and Robert Nurick were invaluable in contributing their technical and substantive expertise during the revision and preparation of the papers for publication. The institute owes a special debt to Reet Varnik, to whom the preparation of the transcripts was entrusted. Subsequently she prepared summaries of the discussions and had the responsibility of making many of the initial revisions on the papers. Her considerable editorial talents are deeply appreciated.

A central role in our efforts was played by the institute's director of programs, Seweryn Bialer, who designed the broad intellectual structure of the enterprise and provided the intellectual impetus for it, and by the assistant director of the institute, Sophia Sluzar, who contributed creatively to the intellectual format and also supplied the indispensable organizational leadership. Without them, this series would not have been realized.

The institute also wishes to acknowledge and to thank the National Endowment for the Humanities for providing partial funding for the workshops.

Zbigniew Brzezinski

Radical Visions
of the Future

Leszek Kolakowski, professor of the history of philosophy at the University of Warsaw until 1968, was dismissed from that position during a wave of cultural and academic repression. Currently a senior research fellow at All Souls College, Oxford, Professor Kolakowski has been a visiting professor of philosophy at Yale University, McGill University, and the University of California at Berkeley. Among his numerous works on philosophy, religion, and culture are Marxism and Beyond, The Devil and Scripture, *and* The Socialist Idea: A Reappraisal, *which he coedited. His most important book is* Chrétiens sans Eglise, *published in 1969.*

1

Introduction:
Need of Utopia, Fear of Utopia
Leszek Kolakowski

In trying to introduce several authors' comments on various aspects of utopian thought I should refrain, I believe, from engaging in direct polemics with them. That I do not share many of the opinions expressed in the following essays will be immediately obvious.

It is easy to notice that the word "utopia" may be and is being used in two opposite meanings, both of which are in keeping with its original sense. Sometimes we mean a "place which is nowhere" *yet* but might appear, and sometimes we mean a "place which is nowhere" because it cannot ever exist. We often call "utopian" all human dreams about a better world. In this sense the question "Do we need utopias?" seems pointless, since people have always been thinking about something better than what is now, and it is hard to imagine that they could ever dispense with all anticipations of a better future. Normally, however, we mean a literary genre which portrays a world that is not simply better than the existing one but which is truly perfect, and which suggests that such a world is really possible. If we apply the adjective "utopian" to any idea implying that human affairs can be

improved, the word is useless; such an idea obviously under-
lies all sorts of technological and social planning. And so, the
question "Do we need utopias?" makes sense only if what is
meant are visions of a world in which evil is entirely done
away with, all human values and desires reconciled and effectively materialized—briefly, *summum bonum* incarnate.

To question the need for utopias is a recent habit. Until
our century, utopias might have seemed harmless fantasies
of some literati. However, two factors have emerged which
have made utopias suspect and equivocal. First, it has become
more and more evident that attempts to build the perfect
world of communism have been a disastrous failure. Second,
the idea of "progress" revealed its contradictory character
once people began to realize that almost every step in technological and social development is paid for with a heavy
price, and they started asking themselves under what conditions the price becomes really intolerable. It appears that
technical progress does not necessarily enhance those values
we used to think of as the most precious and may even bring
them into mortal danger. The new literary genre, antiutopias,
is an invention of our century; those who inaugurated it—
Huxley, Zamiatin, Orwell—expressed the increasing fear that
the utopian hopes, when tried in practice, are likely to turn
our world either into hell or, at the best, into a pseudo-
paradise out of which everything which made us human—
creativity, love, imagination—would be banned forever.
Next to negative utopias we have retrospective utopias as
well—dreams of the Great Retreat to a world which is happily
unaware of today's insoluble dilemmas and catastrophic
expectations.

The common sense argument in favor of utopian thinking
is that we must anticipate things that are impracticable now
in order to make them practicable one day in the future. This
argument for the social usefulness of utopias might be valid,
yet the scope of its validity is perhaps limited. It is valid
when applied to technological utopian imagination, a genre
which started with Campanella and Cyrano de Bergerac
(or perhaps even with Roger Bacon) to become a popular

variant of the contemporary science fiction. It is far from obvious, though, that the same argument is equally strong in assessing the role of all-encompassing or "global" utopian thinking.

Optimistic technological utopias derived from a faith in progress which was inherited from the Enlightenment; "global" utopias, however, are modern versions of the Jewish and early Christian apocalyptic literature, extensions of late mediaeval chiliastic dreams. Both their content and their philosophical background are significantly different. It is misleading to use the word "utopia" in a sense which puts in the same category the writings of Jules Verne and the prophecies of Joachim of Fiore. One of the differences is between the belief in progress and the vision of discontinuity of time. "Progress" means continuity, growth, and a series of advances which accumulate in time. To believe in progress is simply to expect that mankind would, step by step, through all sorts of reforms and improvements, make its lot better, increase human control of nature, and abolish war, misery, and oppression. The belief in progress is a natural ally of reformist, utilitarian, rationalist, and technologically-oriented social philosophy. It implies that future advancements will grow on the basis of the progress hitherto achieved.

Not so the "global" apocalyptic utopias of the perfect world. History is portrayed as catastrophic, not evolutionary, and past history, in many important respects, a degradation rather than an upgrowth. There is radical discontinuity between the world as it is and as it will be; a violent leap is needed to do away with the past; a new time will start. Mankind has to descend into hell before the coming of the great day of resurrection, when everything will be fresh and young. The new society is not to be a continuation of the existing one, it will be something *novissimum*, a break with the past. At the same time, new meaning will be given to the past as well.

We may reflect upon the utopian mentality (in this restricted sense) both in psychological and in social terms. It is tempting to say that, psychologically, there is in utopian mentality a quality of adolescence, an image of the world which seems to be entirely open and perfectly malleable. This is a frequent and perhaps natural world perception among young people who are about to start their adult life with a feeling that everything is before them, everything is possible, that the future is open and limitless. We may perhaps interpret the utopian mentality psychoanalytically as an adolescent fixation, but I am not going to venture into this sort of speculation. In social terms, it seems that the spread of catastrophic-utopian thinking expresses despair, rather than hope, or perhaps the attempt to get rid of despair by mythological means. When the order of inherited values is crumbling and the society, for one reason or another, seems to have become stuck in a cul-de-sac, mille-narian fantasies are likely to appear.

This catastrophic approach to history, the expectation of a new time and of a violent break which opens the way to the rebirth of mankind, can be found in most of what we used to call the utopian literature of the nineteenth century, including the writings of Marx. We follow Marx's desperate search for proof that the history of capitalism is a continuous degradation of the working class and that it is bound to be such; Marx believed that, despite all the technological progress, human history has so far been characterized by an increasing alienation of labor, and consequently, by spiritual degradation. We may speak of "progress" not in the sense of continuous improvement, but rather in the sense that the miseries of the past were necessary to bring closer the future Kingdom of Freedom. The whole past pilgrimage of humanity gets its meaning from the future. To be this kind of a meaning-giving source, the future has already to be there. And indeed, in Marx's eyes, and in those of all utopians, the future is there; it is not something just predicted or anticipated, it is a reality after the Hegelian fashion; it's something that cannot be seen empirically and yet is more real than any empirical facts.

The mythological idea of the new time takes another shape, to be sure, when it abandons its specifically religious form. Those Christian sectarians who believed or still believe in the imminence of the Second Coming did not make claims to be initiated in a special technique supposed to bring about the new era; they expected it as a gift of the Holy Ghost. Yet the utopians claim precisely to have mastered the know-how in the domain of the Apocalypse. Whoever is the lucky owner of the spell is entitled, of course, to employ all means to get access to the magic door. This does not mean that all shareholders of the utopian knowledge are or were preaching violence as the proper way to achieve the great transition; historically, it was obviously not so. But all believed they had discovered a special knowledge of perfect happiness, and that this knowledge was valid irrespective of any empirical inquiry that might be undertaken into the matter.

There were only a few crucial years in the history of modern utopian thinking, roughly between 1839 and 1842. Within these years the following works, among others, came out: Proudhon's *Qu'est-ce que la Propriété?;* Weitling's *Die Menschheit wie sie ist und wie sie sein sollte, Garantien der Harmonie und Freiheit,* and *Das Evangelium eines armen Sünders;* Cabet's *Voyage en Icarie;* Blanc's *Organisation du travail;* Jean-Jacques Pillot's *Ni châteaux ni chaumières;* and Moses Hess's *Europäische Triarchie.* These, along with Feuerbach's famous book which appeared in the same period, made up both the positive and the negative background of the Marxian philosophy of history. There were various people among utopians. Some were revolutionaries (like Weitling or Pillot), others believed in the irresistible force of their propaganda and example. Some appealed to the Christian tradition and religious motivations (like Saint-Simonians, Cabet, Weitling, Lammenais), others derived their philosophy from the stereotypes of the Enlightenment. Except for Louis Blanc—who, strictly speaking, was not a utopian but rather a forerunner of social democratic reformism and the first theorist of the welfare state—they believed both in a radical break separating the New World from the old one and in an order which was not simply desirable but which embodied the

human "essence" or human calling. The utopian land is not
something people actually want but what they ought to want
in order to be truly human; its content is inferred from the
knowledge of the essence of humanity. This concept of
human essence, as is usually the case in mythological thinking, is descriptive and normative at the same time. It might
well happen that people actually would want something different from, indeed something opposite to, what their
essence requires. This does not matter, though. Those with
deeper insight into the real (as opposed to false) human needs
know better. The utopian land is a place were this genuine
human essence will coincide with life as it is really lived,
assuring the ultimate harmony of the species. If people refuse to join the enlightened in the journey to paradise, they
have to join them anyway under coercion—though this will
not be coercion, properly speaking, since nothing which aims
to make people truly human can be wrong.

This unconsciously platonic belief that the essence of
humanity can be defined theoretically so that the existential aspirations and desires of people are irrelevant to its
definition, explains the hidden readiness of the utopian
mentality to accept despotic means on the way to the
promised land, even though many, indeed most, of the
utopian writers expected their visions to be fulfilled without
violence or coercion. In fact only the most penetrating minds
among them did not shrink from admitting the necessity of
violence in driving mankind to paradise. It should be added
that the seed of the extreme despotism had been discovered
in utopian mentality long before the great utopia could be
tested in the practice of communism (an experience which is
normally shrugged off by utopians on the assumption that
the testing ground was improperly chosen by history). Most
anarchist critics of communism (including Sorel) pointed
out that the seemingly innocuous fantasies of benevolent
utopian mankind-lovers would fatefully end in a gruesome
tyranny if applied in practice.

The utopian thinkers, once they discovered the genuine
essence of man and once they convinced themselves that

they knew what people wanted without asking them, had to assume that the world was entirely malleable, and that the perfectibility of human species was limitless. They have been almost organically incapable of asking themselves whether their proposals were consistent, i.e., whether all the values they have preached could be materialized together, and whether some conditions, independent of human will, might impose limits on our idea of perfection. It has never occurred to the utopians that some values they have preached are incompatible for empirical reasons and could be implemented only by limiting each other, in difficult compromises and concessions; that perfect equality is imaginable only in conditions of extreme despotism and that people will never be fully equal and fully free at the same time; or that we cannot expect a society where everything is planned and everything spontaneous at the same time. The utopian minds shrink from thinking about limits imposed on our efforts by our biological structure, or by the burdens of the past. They can hardly admit that people have bodies or that they are continuously shaped by the whole of the foregoing human culture. They tend to imagine that the ("true") human history can be initiated afresh, from point zero. Utopia is a blessed land of milk and honey for the human intellect.

One reason why all utopias are bound to be defeated when tested is that the utopian mentality is unable to devise any rational strategy in thinking of the *Terra Nova*. Any rational strategy implies that if we do not know some important elements of the situation in which we operate, we should assume the worst and not the best variant among many possibilities; otherwise we will inevitably lose, if not on the first, then on the second try. This rule appears obvious, yet it is alien to the utopian mentality. Since we do not know enough about our condition, since we cannot be sure what in the evil of the world comes from contingent historical events and what is rooted in lasting properties of human constitution, we are certain losers if we assume in advance that these unknown factors invariably favor our dreams.

It is easy to imagine a society of perfect equality on the assumption that all people are in fact very similar and equally endowed; it is more troublesome if we suppose that some built-in inequalities cannot be eradicated. It is easy to plan universal brotherhood on the assumption that there is nothing in the genetic stock of human species that favors aggressiveness, the desire for domination over other people, or the desire for distinguishing oneself, and that, if such phenomena do appear in human life, this is only because the factories are not yet state owned. It is less easy to plan perfect fraternity if we have reasons to suspect aggressiveness, conflicts, and desire for power and domination have causes which go beyond historical accidents. Rational strategy suggests that we should think of the future on the assumption that the unknown or little known factors relevant to our success are worse, rather than better, in terms of our goals. The utopian mentality is above this sort of consideration. It implies that the existing world is so hopelessly corrupt that it cannot be improved at all, only destroyed root and branch. At the same time, it assumes the most optimistic variant of the conditions which make the New World possible. This is why there is a strong tendency in the utopian mentality to believe that one can institutionalize fraternity, that a community of universal friendship can be brought about by a special social technique.

Still, something worse might happen and indeed seems to have happened to the utopian mentality. We see that utopians, under the pressure of criticism concerning the content of utopia, have escaped into utopias without content. It is a frequent habit of today's cerebral revolutionaries to say: we cannot predict what the future will invent, it would be silly to define the world which does not exist yet; the point is to have a technique to bring this world about. In other words: the utopian mentality can give up any content and be satisfied with a search for technique of the conquest of power. This empty technique is all that remains of the dream.

Is there anything dangerous now in the utopian thinking? Not in the sense that utopians could ever come to power. The place of utopian thinking today is not in established communism, for its adherents are not dreamers; they want power, and they now share very few illusions about the future world of universal happiness. Rather, the place of utopian thinking today is in various leftist sects, which are unable to gain an upper hand in the power struggle, but which are able under certain special conditions to destabilize the political situation and help less utopian forces, whether right or left, to win and to destroy the utopians themselves.

This having been said, is there anything to say in support of utopian thinking? Everything, if the meaning of the word is somewhat restricted. If utopia means a set of highest values we want to defend and to see implemented in social life, nothing prevents us from hanging on to all of them even if we know that they will never be perfectly compatible with each other. If utopia is a regulative idea of the optimum and not an assurance that we have mastered the skill to produce the optimum, then utopia is a necessary part of our thinking. But it would be a puerile fancy to pretend that we know how the world can get rid of scarcity, suffering, hatred, and injustice; nobody knows that. It is safer not to imitate Hitler who promised that in his Germany every girl would find a husband. Whatever can be done in softening scarcity, hatred, and conflicts can be done only in specific points, on a specific scale, by inches. That this should be so is unacceptable to the genuine utopian mentality which looks for the vision of the Last Day, the great leap, the final battle; everything else seems (and is, indeed) grey, boring, lacking pathos, and requiring specific knowledge instead.

It is unlikely, however, that utopian thinking as such could ever be eradicated in our culture. Utopia is a desperate desire to attain absolute perfection; this desire is a degraded remnant of the religious legacy in nonreligious minds. By contrasting the sacred with the profane, mythological order enabled people to accept the inevitable imperfection of the finite world. Once the realm of the sacred collapses in people's minds, the desire for the absolute does not wither away and takes a self-contradictory ideological form; it becomes an idea of the finite and corruptible reality which embodies infinite and incorruptible values. Self-contradictory as it is, this idea might play a useful role insofar as it reveals the imperfection of the existing world, provided that we do not pretend to know how the "absolute" can be constructed here and now.

Robert Nisbet, formerly vice-chancellor of academic affairs at the University of California at Riverside, is currently Albert Schweitzer Professor of History at Columbia University. Also a professor of sociology, Dr. Nisbet has authored numerous works which have an interdisciplinary focus, including Social Change and History, The Social Philosophers: Conflict and Crisis in Western Thought, The Sociological Tradition, *and* The Contribution of Emile Durkheim. *He co-edited with Robert K. Merton the excellent study* Contemporary Social Problems.

2

The Function of the Vision of the Future in Radical Movements

Robert Nisbet

Much of the intellectual ground for the permanent core of radicalism in the nineteenth and twentieth centuries was formed in the eighteenth century as the result of two significant changes in the contemplation of the Golden Age.

Prior to the eighteenth century the Golden Age had been for the most part either an imagined epoch of the remote past or had been cast in religious-millenarian terms for a future that was necessarily transhistorical. In secular thought, at least since Hesiod's *Works and Days* of the eighth century B.C., the Golden Age had been separated from man's hope by a process of continuing and irreversible degeneration that had begun in some aboriginal conflict between felicity and property—with all the psychological states of covetousness and egoistic ambition which were associated with private property. However, in the eighteenth century, the Golden Age became securely moved from distant past to more or less distant future. Moreover, it was thought by a rising number of philosophers that this Golden Age of the future could already be seen beginning to emerge from the womb of the present and that continuing emergence would be made certain by the operation of certain natural laws which, as

Descartes had declared, were invariable though all ages.[1]

Side by side with this transposition of the Golden Age from past to future went another, hardly less momentous change: the secularization of the millenarian state of mind that had been a part of Christianity at least since the thought of Augustine and that had manifested itself in so many sporadic revolts by the apocalyptically-minded in the late Middle Ages. This secularization of the millenarian mind would become incandescent during the French Revolution.

Both changes are closely connected with the history of the idea of progress. This idea had emerged in modern form in the late seventeenth century, a consequence of the famous Quarrel of the Ancients and Moderns. There, however, the idea was limited to knowledge. Defenders of the Moderns believed—seriously, it appears—in the superiority of their own contemporary philosophers, artists, and writers to those of the great ages of Greece and Rome. Little if anything, though, was said then about either human happiness or the general condition of mankind. Preoccupation with knowledge took precedence over the state of society. It is in the eighteenth century, on both sides of the English Channel, and in America, that the idea was extended to such matters as human institutions and human happiness. Much of eighteenth century thought was given to the demonstration of Progress, its epochs in the past, its workings in the present, and its necessity in the future.[2]

Progress, it is fair to say, replaced Providence for the intellectual mind. Turgot's career is a striking example of this replacement. He had entered the Sorbonne as a theology student, with the Church his intended career. A brilliant student, he had been elected *Prieur* by his fellow students, with the obligation to present publicly an occasional discourse. In 1750 he gave two discourses. The first, in July, was "On the Advantages which the Establishment of Christianity has Procured for the Human Race." Here is God in the saddle, though the attentive reader will not miss the rising emphasis toward the end upon purely human causes of Progress. In December of the same year Turgot delivered a second discourse, "A Philosophical Review of the Successive Advances of the Human Mind." Here God has been pretty well retired from the scene. The spirit of Progress has taken over. "May it endure forever, may it extend over all the earth! May men continue to advance along the pathway of truth! Even more, may they become ever better and happier!" It is not surprising to learn that in the following year Turgot abandoned all thought of serving the Church and entered into the quarter-century of government administration for which he is famous.[3]

After Turgot the conception of Progress with its implicit vision of a golden future was made the subject of ever more systematic statement. To give certitude to Progress was the great aim of the late eighteenth century as it was indeed of the nineteenth. In Kant's "Idea of a Universal History," published in 1784, we are treated to the progress of mankind over a vast period of time as a process made inevitable by the very nature of man and of the social order.

A number of other works, written in different parts of Europe during the latter half of the eighteenth century, could be usefully cited and quoted, among them those of Rousseau, Adam Ferguson, Herder, and not least another essay of Turgot, on Universal History, all of which set forth the progressive view of the future.[4] I shall limit myself, however, to brief mention of Condorcet's "Historical Sketch of the Progress of the Human Mind," written in 1793 while he was in hiding from the Jacobin police. Here the past and present of mankind are set forth in nine sequential, genetically related stages of advancement from primitivism. This advancement, Condorcet stresses, has proceeded from the beginning through uniform, natural causes which lie in the very nature of man and of man's relationships with his fellows. Progress has been, in short, inexorable and necessary. So, too, Condorcet declares, will be mankind's advance, already begun, into the next and final stage of human history, the tenth— that which stretches endlessly into the future and represents, as it were, man's liberation from the struggle upward and the beginning of his true history. This history will be a history of the ever-widening achievement of equality. The future, Condorcet writes, can be seen even now in terms of three sovereign principles: "the destruction of inequality between nations; the progress of equality within one and the same nation; and, finally, the real perfecting of mankind."[5]

Moreover, it is all ordained. The same causes which operated to lift humanity from the first to the second stage, and to each one thereafter, continue to operate in accordance with the Cartesian principle of the invariability of nature's laws, and will go on operating throughout the rest of time.

> Everything points to the fact that we are verging upon the epoch of one of the great revolutions of the human race. What can better instruct us as to what to expect from this, or offer us a surer guide for conduct through the midst of its convulsions, than the picture of those revolutions which have preceded and which have prepared the way for it?[6]

The second change affecting contemplation of the future is closely related to the replacement of Providence by Progress. It is the increasing secularization during the eighteenth century of the whole spirit of millenarianism. By this I mean specifically the transposition to this earth of the state of eternal bliss that in earlier Christian thought had been reserved for the heavenly hereafter, itself contingent upon destruction of the earth and everything on it. The Puritan Revolution in the seventeenth century, especially in the Fifth Monarchy movement, had provided transition from the heavenly to the earthly view of apocalyptic redemption. The Fifth Monarchy men expected this final and fulfilling regime to begin almost immediately. "The rule of the saints," Guenter Lewy writes in his excellent *Religion and Revolution*, "would begin in England and spread to the rest of the world." In a pamphlet written in 1653, John Rogers predicted that by 1660 the Fifth Monarchy would have reached Rome and by 1666 it would be visible "over all the earth."[7]

Despite the oft-stated belief in our contemporary histories

that millenarianism disappeared in the rationalist eighteenth century, it did not. It can be seen in Methodist and other forms of "enthusiasm," some of them decidedly radical in social implication. Millenarianism is, though, most vivid in the French Revolution once it was well under way. It was this, Edmund Burke thought, that made the French Revolution different from any revolution or uprising that had ever taken place and that promised continuing "tremors" and "earthquakes" in the political world as far ahead as one could see. More than half a century later, Tocqueville would seize upon this same religious quality as the perspective within which to make sufficient analysis. There is, I would suggest, every reason to make the French Revolution a chapter in the religious history, as well as the political and social histories, of the West. A great deal of the ecstasy that had come to seize the Fifth Monarchy men and others before the Puritan Revolution died out can be seen clearly enough in Jacobin thought and action, especially in some of the texts, tracts, and decrees of the Committee on Public Safety (the word "safety" probably better rendered as "salvation").

Crane Brinton stressed many years ago, in his detailed study of the Jacobins, their backgrounds and interests, along with proclivities and passions, the deeply religious strain that lay in their mentalities. They were, Brinton says, and so regarded themselves, successors to the Puritans of the English revolution, in spirit if not in actual religious membership.[8] Robespierre, whom Condorcet had likened to a "volcano encased in ice," was a deeply pious man, and there should have been no surprise whatever at the time when he and a few others took the initiative in establishing a civil religion, one complete with Supreme Being, rite, liturgy, dogma, and prescribed form of worship. Rousseauian in intellectual origin that religion may be, but in Jacobin hands it took on the distinct character of the millenarianism that more often goes with ecstatic religion than with rationalist philosophy.

In his *Age of Revolution*, Robert Palmer has emphasized the religious character of the Revolution and the religious enshrinement of both present and future.

Revolutionary religion expressed itself spontaneously in many ways, with the forms usually patterned on the Catholicism in which the revolutionaries were brought up. The most passionate Jacobins called the revolution the "sacred sickness" meaning no irony and spoke of Republican temples, martyrs, preachers, hymns, sermons, catechisms and decalogues.[9]

Robespierrian linkage of virtue and terror could only have been effected in what is hardly less than religious frenzy.

From Robespierre it is only a short step, really, to Babeuf; not the Babeuf of the *Plebeian Manifesto,* which he came to renounce, but the Babeuf who, with almost adoring appreciation of what Robespierre and Saint-Just had begun, could see himself and his followers as part of a continuing revolutionary mission. "We must remember," he declared, commemorating tacitly Robespierre and Saint-Just in the statement, "that we are only the second Gracchi of the French Revolution." The idea of the immediate future as deeply revolutionary, and by virtue of this the indispensable avenue to the greater and lasting future of secular redemption, was a common one among Babouvists. "The French Revolution," wrote Maréchal in his *Manifesto of Equals,* "is only the forerunner of another revolution far greater, far more solemn, which will be the last."[10] How often that thought, suitably adapted to circumstance, would be echoed in the decades following!

It is in the nineteenth century that revolutionary radicalism becomes a fixed part of the Western—and in due time the world—scene. This radicalism is formed by the elements we have just examined, all brought to high degree of intensity and given far greater elaboration. The eighteenth century's rediscovery and transposition of the Golden Age, its search for irreversible laws of movement in history which would make certain attainment of the Golden Age, its replacement of the religious by the secular as the vital context of thought on the Golden Age, and, far from least, its millenarianism manifest in the great Revolution, is all very much part of nineteenth century radicalism.

The more obvious teleological elements of the eighteenth century's rendering of progress from primitivism to final fulfillment are commonly gone in the nineteenth century— though certainly not the corollaries proceeding from these elements. The word "law" becomes more frequently used than the eighteenth century's "spirit" or "principle" in theories of progress and futurism. There is an immense momentum to be seen in the direction of the systematic. Blake's "I must Create a System or be enslaved by another Man's" is as apposite to the nineteenth century as to our own day. "Evolution" and "development" as words begin to vie with "progress" in treatments of change, although that last word remains a very popular one in nineteenth century writing, including Darwin's.[11]

Several differences are worth noting, though. After the eighteenth century rationalist effort at demolition there is surprising recrudescence of religion in the nineteenth century, even in certain radical writings. In terms of sheer volume of sects and cults formed, evangelical movements, tracts, and major theological works, the nineteenth century has to be regarded as one of the major ages of religious expression in the West.[12]

But science also becomes the subject of immense adoration, lay as well as intellectual, as we know. Raymond Williams in his *Culture and Society, 1780-1950,* notes that among the plethora of words either coined or endowed with new meanings in the early part of the century are "scientist" and "science," with the latter's common referent the physical and natural disciplines but extending nevertheless to any body of knowledge, including the social, to which certitude could be given.[13] By the middle of the century the word "science" was to be found in many areas of writing, almost always treated reverentially.

Given the almost equal veneration in the century for religion and science, it is not surprising that their marriage should have been effected in many quarters. Insensibly the conception of a scientific religion, and also of a religion of

science, began to spread. Mary Baker Eddy was just as convinced, as were her followers, that she had for the first time
in history made religion scientific as Marx and his followers
were that they had made study of past, present, and future
scientific. If the aim of science was, in Comte's word, "prevision,"[14] so was the aim of a great deal of evangelical religion in the nineteenth century prevision of, and also preparation for, the future. Given its underpinnings by religion and science alike, the future was bound to achieve in
that century a degree of luminosity it never had before or
since. Through whatever means, the future was well within
human grasp. So it was thought and written.

There is greater particularization of the future in the
nineteenth than the eighteenth century. There "felicity"
commonly sufficed as description of man's future state.
Later, however, the future was filled in technologically and
institutionally. Almost universally, radicals in the nineteenth
century embraced the new technology, industrialism, commerce, trade, and the city as harbingers of the future. Private
property and profit were to be obliterated, or sharply
reduced, but all the fundamental structures of industrialism
were sanctified and projected into the golden future. It was
to conservatives one had to go to get indictments of technology, factory, city, and spoliation of the countryside.[15]

But the integrating and classificatory role of the imagined
future in division of the present between the "relevant" and
the "irrelevant" was very great. How else, after all, was a
philosopher of either revolution or evolution to dismiss one
large part of the present, the institutional present, as being
but a congeries of the archaic and obsolete and to endow
another part of the present with the magic word "progressive" or "modern," except in light of prior faith in what the
Golden Age would actually consist of?[16]

Revolution is hard work, as one of Silone's characters
expresses it. It is also dangerous work, or used to be. And
finally it is difficult work—knowing what is strategic, what
is real, what is objective, what course to take in terms of long
run action. What else but a contemplation of the future that

is at once millenarian and scientific—in imagination at least—can guide those who labor in the vineyards of revolution? One may grant that precipitating forces in revolutionary behavior are more likely to be situational—to be direct results of perceptions of collapsed values and standards of living, of strong feelings of contrast between what is promised by a social and political order and what is actually delivered, and of insights into the actual strength of a political regime. But while this is true, it is no less true that actions, judgements, and strategies grow and proliferate in benign climates. For revolutionary thought in the nineteenth century, the Golden Age—set securely in the future and given solid undergirding by such intellectual elements in philosophy and science as necessity, iron trends of event and circumstance, and directionality—was a very benign climate indeed. It is more than coincidence that the century in which the idea of revolution was brought to almost religious intensity was also the century in which the idea of progress flourished.

The future, its correct reading and analysis, was very important to the minds of those who, in addition to their revolutionary and messianic ambitions, cherished the dream of founding for the first time in history a genuine social science. Saint-Simon, Comte, Marx, Proudhon, and Fourier all took very seriously their roles as makers of a true science of society. The fundamental aim of science, Comte wrote early in the century, is "prevision," a word in which he neatly combined prediction, as understood in the physical sciences, with prophecy as understood in religion.

There were a few in the nineteenth century whose conception of a social science was based upon analysis of present and past without illusion of being able to offer insight into the future. Le Play and George Cornewall Lewis are two who come to mind. But there were not many of these. Among the larger number, certainly among the more illustrious, the future exerted strong appeal upon the makers of social science. One studied past and present primarily for intellectual capture of the trends which, it was hardly doubted, would carry man into the golden future.

Vision of the future had, in sum, strong effect upon the way the present was not merely thought about but actually perceived. As noted above, the future once glimpsed made it easy to divide the present into the "relevant" and the "irrelevant" present, into that which augurs and becomes a part of the future and that which is but residue of the past. The doctrine of survivals was conceived to make possible consignment of large segments of the present to the past. A whole new rhetoric came into being, overwhelmingly political in thrust. Such words as "folk," "traditional," "survival," "reactionary," and "conservative" became overnight words of invective, justified by ultimate reference to the future.[17] And at the opposite extreme such words as "progressive," "forward-looking," "liberal," and "radical" took on their increasingly popular flavor from the fact that in these the whole thrust was toward the future. The fact that the future cannot in fact be forecast did not have the slightest effect upon belief that it could. Past equalled bad, present good, and future best. Each of the system-builders—Saint-Simon, Comte, Fourier, Marx, et al.—invariably looked with contempt upon those whose conceptions of the future were "unscientific," that is, objectively unrealistic.[18]

One striking element of the present repudiated almost uniformly by the radicals insofar as the future was concerned was the political state. Technology, city, commerce and trade, even the factory—suitably decontaminated—could all seem vital elements of the wave of the future, their criticism the mere exhalation of reaction, but the line was drawn when it came to that most modern of institutions, the centralized national state. However awesome the implications of power are in Saint-Simon's New Christianity, in Fourier's vast complex of phalansteries (each a monolith containing some 1800 persons), or in what may be inferred from Marx and Engels on the shape of the future, there is yet dislike of the state and widespread belief that it will have eroded or been destroyed before the Golden Age begins. Saint-Simon and Comte are extremely critical of the kind of state that the Jacobins had brought into being, as well as of the Napoleonic order. Marx, as we know, thought the abolition of classes would lead in time to abolition of the state, though his and Engels' words in the *Manifesto* on "all production . . . concentrated in the hands of the vast association of the whole nation," and their recommended measures of centralization and monopolization of key industries, were among the many which rubbed raw the disciples of Proudhon and Bakunin. It is in anarchist writing that the most luminous vision of a future devoid of the national state is to be found.[19]

But however the future might be particularized and given historical thrust, its color was dominantly gold in the radical mind throughout the century. Saint-Simon's eloquent words are pertinent:

> The imagination of poets has placed the golden age in the cradle of the human race. It was the age of iron they should have banished there. The golden age is not behind us, but in front of us. It is the perfection of social order. Our fathers have not seen it; our children will arrive there one day, and it is for us to clear the way.[20]

To clear the way! In no respect did the optimistic vision of the future affect radical policy and strategy more crucially than by the inference drawn that wisdom lay not in trying to fashion the good society but, rather, in clearing the track of all historical debris in order that society would make its own way to goodness. Granted that there were some such as Fourier and also Proudhon who devoted a good deal of writing to the more or less exact nature of the future, there was still confidence that the laws of history were inexorable and that the future would emerge from the present if only history were allowed to reach its eventual station.

The immense popularity of the railroad after about 1830 supplied rich metaphor in this respect. Tennyson, who took his first ride in 1830 on the train from Liverpool to Manchester and who was under the impression that the wheels ran in grooves, wrote in the poem "Locksley Hall": "Let the great world spin forever down the ringing grooves of change." Tennyson was no radical, but the image of the train and its locomotive, its tracks, and its stations was a popular one in radical and liberal thought alike, as well it might have been, given the largely unilinear conception of history that existed and the confidence—nowhere greater than among radicals—that the West was the vanguard of mankind, its path or track the one all peoples would in time get on.

The final summary observation I want to make before mentioning in vignette fashion a few of the principals in the radical quest for the future has to do with the prestige that *communality* acquired. Communalism is, with rarest exceptions, the shape of the future for the radical mind of the nineteenth century. This is just as true of Saint-Simon and Comte and Fourier as it is of Proudhon and Marx and their successors. Nor can we overlook the occasional hint of belief in some aboriginal state of communalism from which there had been evolutionary emergence, if not actually "Fall." This is certainly present in Marx. In his Paris writings, the account of alienation carries with it the implication that prior to man's alienation from self and fellows, which is to say, prior to the rise of private property, something in the way of wholeness of the human spirit had existed. Marxian dislike of private property and its attendant vices is fully the equal of Hesiod's or Seneca's. Only the abolition of private property can lead to the abolition of all forms of alienation, Marx tells us. In *The German Ideology* there is the idyll of communism given where men will hunt in the morning, fish in the afternoon, etc. This from the Marx who but three years later in the *Manifesto* would refer to the "idiocy of rural life"!

I turn now to a few brief examples of the different ways the future as Golden Age could serve present aspirations among radical minds and movements in the nineteenth century. I shall begin with Saint-Simon, who is probably the first to sanctify industrialism, to see it as the natural and necessary emergent of the evolutionary past, and to endow it with millennial intensity. I turn next to Fourier, whose thought was fully as evolutionary in character as Saint-Simon's, but who—together with followers—sought to commence immediately the actual building of the future, through constructions of his celebrated phalansteries and analogous communities. Third, there is Proudhon and his fusion of Progress and Revolution together with systematic analysis of the economic and political changes which must be effected in the present industrial-political system in order that the future may be *made* as well as merely be the result of developmental principles. And, finally, I shall mention Sorel and his idea of fabrication of the future. (I am passing over Marx here inasmuch as Marxism is the subject of other papers in this volume.)

"The future belongs to us," exulted Saint-Simon, surrounded by a few disciples just before his death. He believed that it must be brought into being through organization of the working classes. He said: "Our intention is to promote and explain the inevitable,"[21] and it was his merit, keeping sharp eye on the present, to set the inevitable in a strongly evolutionary context. Following a thought of Turgot's, and in advance of Comte, Saint-Simon dealt with mankind's development in terms of the intellectual stages of religion, metaphysics, and science—the latter just coming into view in his own day and giving preview of the universal mentality of man in the future—and of social stages commencing in the slavery of the ancient world, passing through feudalism and culminating in industrialism. He worshipped industry, by which he meant humanely governed factories and all that went with them in the way of production, but also a whole way of life and thought that would be rooted in rational technique. It was Saint-Simon who coined the verb "industrialize," and he did not doubt that it was the mission of the working class, through organization, to industrialize the world. What he came in time to call the New Christianity was one purged of supernationalism and rooted in the whole industrial-technical complex. In 1817 he adopted the motto: "Everything by industry, everything for industry." For him the nation was no more than "a great industrial society," and politics reduced itself basically to "the science of production."[22] He sometimes seems a prophet of the past in his passion for mediaeval values of organic order, but there is no mistaking either his devotion to the future or the context of historical necessity in which he set achievement of the future.[23]

What he began others continued, among them Charles Fourier and Auguste Comte. Fourier seems to have gone to his grave in the belief that his "law of the passions" was his greatest contribution to mankind. Its true importance lies, however, in its theoretical underpinning of what plainly fascinated him most: anticipation of the future by positive and immediate establishment of phalansteries—immense buildings within which phalanges would exist as substitutes for the obsolete family, and which would become the real communities of life, liberty, and the pursuit of happiness. Private property is not actually abolished by Fourier, but the elaborate system of shares he decrees, with a kind of guaranteed annual wage for each person, comes close enough to its abolition. Hesiodic fear of private property as the root of evil, united with the Christian view of heaven as the final liberation of man from all the torments of egoism, is, in short, very much a part of Fourierism.[24]

No one who has studied the wave of utopian communalism that exists in the nineteenth century side by side with the waves of religious revival and of scientism can doubt the impress on otherwise practical minds of the ideas of Fourier. It is important to realize that these people who left their communities of birth to go, often at great distances, to new areas where their utopias could be instituted, were almost unanimous in their conviction that what they were doing was bringing the future into existence. The most bizarre or for that matter utilitarian of ideas for living in the present could be justified by proper invoking of the future.

Organization was the thing! In the writings of Saint-Simon, Fourier, and Comte alike is the insistence that organizations must be brought into existence immediately to give guidance to those trends which were gradually and inexorably bringing the future into ken. Converts must be found, energies stimulated, loyalties mobilized, actual examples created, in order to make the future a vivid reality as quickly as possible. Thus the establishment, so often with pathetic results, of communities in New England, New Jersey, Texas, Illinois, and California (where, at one time, several dozen of them existed, each intoxicated by the thought of anticipation of the future).[25]

This contemplation of the future affected no one more than Proudhon. It would be hard to find any mind, I think, more steeped in the idea of progress, whether conceived in terms of historical principle running through all of time or of actual specification of the way in which the future should be prepared for and actually brought into existence. May I say

(May I say parenthetically that as historians we can welcome the recent signs of revival of interest in this extraordinary man. Back in the 1930s, as some of us will recall, one could stamp himself a simpleton among radicals if he spoke well of Proudhon. For was it not true, Marxists asked peremptorily, that Proudhon had been forever destroyed for the fool he was by Marx's *Poverty of Philosophy?* A brave soul was required to answer the question in the negative.

Playing for the moment that most demanding of historian's games known as *IF*, I would argue that had the Franco-Prussian war gone differently, there is excellent reason for believing that Proudhonian rather than Marxian socialism would have entered the twentieth century triumphant. Marx himself, in a letter just before the outbreak of that war, expressed the hope that the French would be thrashed, for then, he argued, the center of gravity of socialism would pass from France to Germany where it belonged. And Marx was proved right by the actual course of events.[26])

In Proudhon there is rich if frequently confused combination of philosophy of history and of serious concern with the kind of society that would best represent creative use of the key elements of production and political authority. He had the same regard for industry that other radicals in the century had, but he also carried to the end his belief in landscape and the necessity of balance between the urban and the rural, the technological and the natural. And to a degree far above most of his contemporaries he feared power, particularly centralized power, and especially in its nationalistic-democratic forms. Fanciful though his explorations of mutualism may be, his effort actually to conceive some of the operating details of a syndicalist-plural society took from socialism the kind of deadly and sterile determinism that in the Marxist tradition was to culminate in Lenin and Stalin.

Proudhon did, however, have an almost mystical regard for the principle of progress. "What dominates all my studies . . . is that resolutely and irrevocably, in all things and everywhere, I proclaim Progress."[27] He denounced the "absolute," but it is not hard to see in Proudhon's treatment of the principle of progress the same kind of absolutism that we find in most other evolutionary avenues to the future. In 1843, in his *Creation,* he declared, almost in Comte's words, that the law of progress is "the mind's upward movement through the three successive stages of Religion, Philosophy and Metaphysics or method, toward Science."[28] Revolution is for Proudhon no more at bottom than the principle of progress manifesting itself from stage to stage in successive approximations of justice.

In the first volume of his *Justice* (1858), he wrote:

> We are not moving toward an ideal perfection or final state that we can attain in a single moment, when at death we cross its boundary. We are carried along with the universe in a constant process of development. The more we develop intellectually, the more certain and glorious this development will be. Progress is therefore the law of our souls.[29]

There is an interesting blend of archaist and futurist in Proudhon. It is hard to miss a certain flavor of traditionalism in his insistence upon the family. The same holds with respect to Proudhon's emphasis upon the commune. Despite Proudhon's hatred of revealed, institutionalized religion, and of hereditary class, there is a strong heritage in his writing of the traditionalism that had flowered in France just after the Revolution.[30]

But the sense of future is as intoxicating to Proudhon as it is to any other nineteenth century radical mind. Redemption lies in making our way as swiftly and expeditiously as possible into the future. This future will be—anarchy. In several places, *The Federal Principle* and *The Philosophy of Progress* preeminently, he offers insight into the nature of anarchism, but nowhere is there better expression of his views on the matter than in a letter written in 1864. Anarchism is

> a form of government or constitution in which public and private consciousness, formed through the development of science and law, is alone sufficient to maintain order and guarantee all liberties. In it, as a consequence, the institutions of police, preventive and repressive methods, officialdom, taxation, etc. are reduced to a minimum. In it, more especially, the forms of monarchy and of intensive centralization disappear, to be replaced by federal institutions and a pattern of life based on the commune.[31]

Equality will prevail, but it must be equality of "means"—that is, of opportunity—not "equality of well-being" which, if enforced, would be a violation of justice and equity.

> When politics and homelife have become one and the same thing, when economic problems have been solved in such a way that individual and collective interests are identical, then—all constraint having disappeared—it is evident that we will be in a state of total liberty or anarchy."[32]

The essential role of the future, and of the idea of progress which comes close to being scriptural in Proudhon, is that of providing continuing inspiration to the working class. That there *is* a benign future, that it will be achieved through the workings of the principle of progress, supplemented by the proliferation of voluntary associations ("multiply your associations and be free!")—none of this Proudhon seems ever to have doubted. For the present the idea of progress "will protect society from both the laziness of conservatism and from false revolutionary enterprises.[33]

I turn now in conclusion to still another vision of the

future, or, rather, a means of utilizing the future as a dynamic myth. For Sorel, in the beginning a conservative (and also an engineer), the greatest enemy of genuine revolution was the intellectual class and all of its rationalizations of evolution, progress, and gradualism. As one reads Sorel, it is evident that what excites his hatred is not so much the idea of *progress* as the *idea* of progress. An admirer of Marx, Sorel came to believe that what was sound and redemptive in Marx had been vulgarized and denatured by the professors, chiefly German, who had become mesmerized by the evolutionary elements in Marxism. Only when the authentic Marx was rescued from the ministrations of his academic followers might a genuinely revolutionary movement be brought into being. The future, far from being a natural and inexorable emergent, must be actually constructed in men's minds.

Sorel's *Illusions of Progress* is one of the most brilliantly perceptive studies of the philosophy of progress to be found in modern writing. "Clowns of a degenerate aristocracy" is Sorel's phrase for the perpetrators of an idea that has, he felt, through its emphasis upon the automatic and continuous character of progress, done all modern thought great damage.[34]

Illusions of Progress was published in 1908, the same year in which appeared also his *Decomposition of Marxism* and his *Reflections on Violence,* without doubt Sorel's three greatest works. They need to be read together, for each is, unless read against the background of the other two, defective in argument.[35] In the *Decomposition of Marxism* Sorel vents his dislike of the whole liberal, gradualist, evolutionary argument which had, in his view, taken from Marx its valuable revolutionary element, steeped in the necessity of violence, and made it into what would surely prove to be an actual shoring-up of capitalism. Sorel scoffs at the idea of capitalism ever disappearing through its supposedly iron laws of internal contradiction. Contradictions (of an intellectual kind) or no, capitalism is capable, Sorel thought, of continuing indefinitely, unless it is destroyed through direct, mounting, and relentless revolutionary action.

As I noted above, Sorel began as a conservative in thought, and his chief dislike was liberalism, not only for its fatuous belief in inevitable progress but for its dissolution of the dogmas on which alone any social order can be made to succeed. Sorel shared Saint-Simon's and Proudhon's contempt for the ideals of unrestricted freedom of speech and thought, devoid of moral limit, seeing these as acids on the necessary fabric of consensus. From Proudhon, Sorel acquired his fondness for *syndicats*—autonomous, or largely autonomous, associations which would combine economic, social, cultural, and political functions. There is little hint of individualism in these. As a conservative, Sorel had written his brilliant defense of the execution of Socrates; Sorel's *Decline of the Ancient World* was also written in the light of his conviction that an effective social order was incompatible with the ideals of individualistic liberalism. His dislike of nationalism, bureaucratized democracy, and centralization, as well as capitalism, is also set in considerable appreciation of Proudhonian mutualism.

Sorel and Proudhon differ on progress. Yet this does not mean in any way a renunciation of the future in Sorel's thinking. On the contrary, it would be hard to find anyone more deeply convinced of the necessity of use of the future—of, in his phrase, "the framing of the future"—for revolutionary activity. His myth of the general strike must of course be seen in this light. Itself the product of Sorel's reflections on Christianity and on the immense value to this religion in its destruction of imperial Rome of rooted belief in the Second Coming, it is nothing if not future-obsessed. Mindful of the criticisms which the idea of the general strike had received, Sorel writes:

> And yet without leaving the present, without reasoning about the future, which seems forever condemned to escape our reason, we should be unable to act at all. Experience shows that *the framing of a future, in some indeterminate time,* may, when it is done in a certain way, be very effective. . . . This happens when the anticipations of the future take the form of those myths which enclose

with them all the strongest inclinations of the mind . . . and
which give an aspect of complete reality to the hopes of immediate action by which, more easily than by any other method, men
can reform their desires, passions and mental activity.[36]

The eschatological quality of Sorel's thinking on revolution, on future, and on social redemption is plain to all
readers. His celebrated doctrine of violence is no more, at
bottom, than a kind of religious recognition of the purifying,
as well as the integrating and eventually liberating, properties of force. For Sorel any creative act, starting with organic
birth, is an inherently violent act. He is no worshipper of
violence as its own end and criticizes harshly the Jacobins
and their "senseless, wanton and opposition-arousing" use
of the guillotine.

Nevertheless violence of some kind is required by the very
nature of man and society. It is, Sorel argues, conservatism,
routine, and habit—rather than change—which are the fundamental elements of mankind. For human beings to be shaken
free of these fetters, violent change is required and is alone
effective. Gradualism in change is for Sorel a contradiction in
terms. Only through widening belief in the millennial certainty of a universal strike in which all workers everywhere
will lay down their tools, and, with this belief, consecration
to the violence necessary to prepare the way, can a golden
age worthy of the name be brought into existence.

In quick summary: throughout Western history, the idea
of the Golden Age has been a profoundly evocative one,
sometimes expressed in religious, sometimes in secular terms.
One of the most momentous changes of the eighteenth
century was the secure transposition of the Golden Age as
evocative symbol from the remote past to the future, the
sometimes imminent future. First detailed in terms of the
arts and sciences only, the Golden Age of the future had become, well before the end of the eighteenth century, the
repository of economic, political, and social virtues. So also
had the Golden Age come to be envisaged as the eventual

outcome of iron tendencies of change embedded in mankind, beyond power of enemies of progress in the long run to arrest or divert. Every bit of this combined utopianism and historical determinism can be seen in Condorcet alone in the eighteenth century.

Nevertheless it is in the nineteenth century that the image of the Golden Age becomes welded into the utopian-revolutionary tradition that has lasted, with modifications, to our own day. It was precisely because such minds as Saint-Simon, Comte, Fourier, Cabet, and Blanc had reached, by 1840, the utterly confident belief that the future lay in the present, that only the strategical or tactical work of *releasing* the future from the present's womb was required—along with, to be sure, occasional detailed descriptions of the future—that the kind of disguised utopianism we know as Marx's "scientific socialism" could ever have come into existence.

As I noted briefly above, the actual *causes* of any given revolution are many and complex, generally rooted for the most part in immediate contexts rather than long-held beliefs about the future or anything else. But this said, it is impossible, I believe, to explain the intensity, the continuity, and the universal appeal of the revolutionary tradition first in Europe, then the world, apart from its anchorage in beliefs of almost religious fervor concerning the future. I do not think it too strong to say that once the myth of the Golden Age had been transposed, as it had been by the year 1800, from past to future, the revolutionary turbulence the world has known ever since was made virtually inevitable.

Bertell Ollman, associate professor in the Department of Politics, New York University, is the author of Alienation: Marx's Conception of Man in Capitalist Society *and of various articles on Marxism in journals in the United States, Britain, and France.*

3

Marx's Vision of Communism:
A Reconstruction

Bertell Ollman

I

Marcuse argues that, in the middle of the twentieth century, utopia remains an impossible dream only to those theorists who use "the concept of 'utopia' to denounce certain sociohistorical possibilities."[1] Every significant advance in wealth, technology, and science extends the boundaries not only of the real but of the possible, of the ways this newly won potential can be realized. Today's production of goods and knowledge, together with accompanying skills, have transformed the utopias of an earlier time into practical alternatives to our everyday existence. Recognition of these trends and their meaning has led to a renewed interest in Marx's vision of the communist society.

Marx construed his vision of communism out of the human and technological possibilities visible in his time, given the priorities that would be adopted by a new socialist society. The programs introduced by a victorious working class to deal with the problems left by the old society and the revolution would unleash a social dynamic whose general results, Marx believed, could be charted beforehand. Projecting the communist future from existing patterns and trends is an integral part of Marx's analysis of capitalism, an analysis which links social and economic problems with the objective interests that incline each class to deal with them in distinctive ways; what unfolds are the real possibilities inherent in a socialist transformation of the capitalist mode of production. It is in this sense that Marx declares, "we do not anticipate the world dogmatically, but rather wish to find the new world through the criticism of the old."[2] Like the projections Marx made of the future of capitalism itself, however, what he foresaw for communism is no more than highly probable. Marx, whose excessive optimism is often mistaken for crude determinism, would not deny that some form of barbarism is another alternative, but a socialist victory—either through revolution or at the polls—is considered far more likely.[3]

Marx's communist society is in the anomalous position of being, at one and the same time, the most famous of utopias and among the least known. And, while no one disputes the importance of Marx's vision of communism in Marxism, the vision itself remains clouded and unclear. Responsibility for this state of affairs lies, in the first instance, with Marx himself, who never offers a systematic account of the communist society. Furthermore, he frequently criticizes those socialist writers who do as foolish, ineffective, and even reactionary. There are also remarks which suggest that one cannot describe communism because it is forever in the process of becoming: "Communism is for us not a stable state which is to be established, an ideal to which reality will have to adjust itself. We call communism the real movement which abolishes the present state of things. The conditions of this movement result from the premises now in existence."[4]

Yet, as even casual readers of Marx know, descriptions of the future society are scattered throughout Marx's writings. Moreover, judging from an 1851 outline of what was to become *Capital*, Marx intended to present his views on communism in a more systematic manner in the final volume. The plan changed, in part because Marx never concluded his work on political economy proper, and what Engels in a letter to

Marx refers to as "the famous 'positive', what you 'really' want" was never written.[5] This incident does point up, however, that Marx's objection to discussing communist society was more of a stategic than of a principled sort. More specifically, and particularly in his earliest works, Marx was concerned to distinguish himself from other socialists for whom prescriptions of the future were the main stock-in-trade. He was also very aware that when people change their ways and views it is generally in reaction to an intolerable situation in the present and only to a small degree because of the attraction of a better life in the future. Consequently, emphasizing communism could not be an effective means to promote proletarian class consciousness, his immediate political objective. Finally, with only the outline of the future visible from the present, Marx hesitated to burden his analysis of capitalism with material that could not be brought into focus without undermining in the minds of many the scientific character of his entire enterprise.

Notwithstanding Marx's own practice and contrary to his implicit warning, in what follows I have tried to reconstruct Marx's vision of communism from his writings of 1844—the year in which he set down the broad lines of his analysis—to the end of his life. Assembling these varied comments the communist society falls into place like the picture on a puzzle. It is a picture in which many pieces are missing and others so vague as to be practically undecipherable. Yet, what is left is a more complete and coherent whole than most people have thought to exist. Despite serious temptations, I have not gone beyond Marx's actual words in piecing together the components of the communist society. Gaps and uncertainties are left untouched. On occasion, however, when all the evidence points to a particular conclusion, I am not averse to naming it.

Is this effort to reconstruct Marx's vision of the future open to the same criticisms that kept Marx from presenting his own views on this subject in a more organized manner? I don't think so. No one today is likely to confuse Marxism, even with the addition of an explicit conception of communism, with other socialist schools whose names are difficult to recall. Whether describing communism can help raise proletarian class consciousness is a more difficult question. There is no doubt in my mind that getting workers to understand their exploitation as a fundamental and necessary fact of the capitalist system, the avowed aim of most of Marx's writings, is the "high road" to class consciousness. It seems equally clear to me that the inability to conceive of a humanly superior way of life, an inability fostered by this same exploitation, has contributed to the lassitude and cynicism which helps to thwart such consciousness. Viewed in this light, giving workers and indeed members of all oppressed classes a better notion of what their lives would be like under communism (something not to be gleaned from accounts of life in present-day Russia and China) is essential to the success of the socialist project.

As for being able to know only the broad outlines of communism, this is as true now as it was in Marx's time. But whereas presenting this outline then could only reflect negatively on Marxism as a whole, this is no longer the case, for the intervening century has brought pieces of Marx's horizon underfoot and made most of the rest—as I have indicated— easier to see and to comprehend. Still general and incomplete, the secret of the future revealed in Marx's masterly analysis of capitalist society is a secret whose time has come, and publicizing it has become another means of bringing the human fulfillment it portrays into existence.

II

Marx divides the communist future into halves, a first stage generally referred to as the "dictatorship of the proletariat" and a second stage usually called "full communism." The historical boundaries of the first stage are set in the following claim: "Between capitalist and communist society lies the period of the revolutionary transformation of the one into the other. There corresponds to this also a political transition period in which the state can be nothing but the revolutionary dictatorship of the proletariat."[6]

The overall character of this period is supplied by Marx's statement:

> What we have to deal with here is a communist society, not as it has developed on its own foundations, but, on the contrary, just as it emerged from capitalist society; which is thus in every respect, economically, morally and intellectually, still stamped with the birthmarks of the old society from whose womb it emerges.[7]

This first stage is the necessary gestation period for full communism; it is a time when the men who have destroyed capitalism are engaged in the task of total reconstruction. As a way of life and organization it has traits in common with both capitalism and full communism and many which are uniquely its own. When its work is done—and Marx never indicates how long this may take—the first stage gives way gradually, almost imperceptibly, to the second.

Our main sources for Marx's views on the dictatorship of the proletariat are the *Communist Manifesto,* the "Critique of the Gotha Program," and "Civil War in France," in which he discusses the reforms of the Paris Commune. In the *Communist Manifesto,* there are ten measures that workers' parties are urged to put into effect immediately after their victory over the capitalists. By viewing these measures as already accomplished, we can use this list as a basis for our picture of the first stage.

What Marx asks for are:

> 1) Abolition of property in land and application of all rents of land to public purposes. 2) A heavy progressive or graduated income tax. 3) Abolition of all rights of inheritance. 4) Confiscation of the property of all emigrants and rebels. 5) Centralization of credit in the hands of the state, by means of a national bank with state capital and an exclusive monopoly. 6) Centralization of communication and transport in the hands of the state. 7) Extension of factories and instruments of production owned by the state, the bringing in cultivation of waste lands, and the improvement of the soil generally in accordance with a common plan.

8) Equal liability of all to labor. Establishment of industrial armies, especially for agriculture. 9) Combination of agriculture with manufacturing industries; gradual abolition of the distinction between town and country, by a more equable distribution of population over the country. 10) Free education for all children in public schools. Abolition of children's factory labor in its present form. Combination of education with industrial production, etc., etc.[8]

It is conceded that "these measures will of course differ in different countries," but in the most advanced countries they "will be pretty generally applicable." No matter the variation in means, and it appears these variations would be modest ones, the goals remain the same: "to wrest . . . all capital from the bourgeoisie, to centralize all instruments of production in the hands of the state . . . and to increase the total of productive forces as rapidly as possible."

These demands will be examined singly in order to reveal the full measure of change projected by each one: "1) Abolition of property in land and application of all rents of land to public purposes." Rather than parceling out estates and giving land to the people who work on it—the reactionary dream of all peasants—land becomes the property of the state, which uses the rent it receives for public purposes. Judging from Marx's treatment of the land question in "Civil War in France," farmers would pay less rent to the state than they paid to their former landlords.[9] Later in his life, faced with Bakunin's criticisms, Marx qualifies this demand:

> The proletariat must take measures, as a government, through which the peasant finds his position directly improved, which thus win him for the revolution; measures, however, which facilitate in nucleus the transition from private property in the soil to collective property, so that the peasant comes to it of his own accord, economically. But it must not antagonize the peasant, by, for instance, proclaiming the abolition of the right of inheritance or the abolition of his property; this is only possible where the capitalist tenant has ousted the peasant, and the real tiller of the soil is just as much a proletarian, a wage worker, as is the urban

worker, and hence has directly, and not only indirectly, the same interests as he. One has even less right to strengthen small peasant property by simply enlarging the plots by the transfer of the large estates to the peasants, as in Bakunin's revolutionary campaign.[10]

This apparent contradiction can be explained by the fact that here Marx is primarily concerned with tactics and with those peasants who work their own plots of land, while in the *Communist Manifesto* he was speaking mainly about non-owning peasants. The two positions can be reconciled as follows: before, during, and immediately after the revolution care should be taken not to frighten the small land-owning peasants, while the landless peasants are to be collectivized at once on the estates of their former landlords and employers. Marx never wavered in his belief that if socialism is to "have any chance whatever of victory, it must at least be able to do as much immediately for the peasants, *mutatis mutandis*, as the French bourgeoisie did in its revolution."[11]

For Marx, the peasant, despite his numerous delusions, is "above all a man of reckoning."[12] He could not fail to be attracted by the tax benefits, material comforts, work conditions, and cultural life available on collectives. These, it would appear, are the arguments that will convince the small-holding peasant to communize his property, without depriving him of anything he already has. Marx did not envision great difficulty in making this transition, nor that it would take much time.

"2) A heavy progressive or graduated income tax." Apparently, significant differences of income still exist at this stage, or, at least, at the start of it. Many enterprises are privately owned, and their owners probably make more than they would working in a factory. Moreover, in a full employment economy with a scarcity of many essential skills, there are still occupations that have to pay high wages in order to attract workers. The inequality of incomes, therefore, is economically necessary, but because it is also socially undesirable an attempt is made through the income tax to render the real gap as narrow as possible. With the increasing equalization of incomes, the progressive income tax soon becomes outmoded.

"3) Abolition of all rights of inheritance." Differences between personal incomes are deplored but accepted as necessary. The disparity in family fortunes, however, is not acceptable, and is to be eliminated at the death of those who currently hold them. Even those modest fortunes which result from wage differentials cannot be bequeathed to one's children. How this is reconciled with the intention, stated earlier, of letting small-holding peasants retain their land until they themselves decide to join collectives is nowhere made clear. Nor do we know for sure what Marx includes among the things which cannot be inherited.

While discussing wages, Marx declares "nothing can pass to the ownership of individuals except individual means of consumption."[13] Something similar, no doubt, would be used to distinguish between what can and cannot be inherited. The purpose of the no-inheritance principle is to achieve wealth equality after the death of those now living. From this time forward, everyone begins life with the same material advantages, and equality of opportunity—an impossible dream under capitalism—is finally realized. What people acquire over and above this will be what they have earned through their own activity.

"4) Confiscation of the property of all emigrants and rebels." This is a practical step intended not so much to aid the state in its drive towards public ownership as to serve as a warning to the bourgeoisie not to engage in counterrevolutionary activity. The proletariat's victory is not completed with the revolution, but must be fought over and won again with all those leftovers of the old society whose hostility impairs the process of social reconstruction. It is indicative of the humanity with which Marx confronts counterrevolutionaries that confiscation is the most severe punishment ever mentioned.

"5) Centralization of credit in the hands of the state, by means of a national bank with state capital and an exclusive monopoly." Carrying this measure into effect will deprive financiers of both their wealth and their power to direct the economy. With exclusive control of credit facilities, the state can decide what parts of the economy should be expanded and by how much. It will also enable the state to finance the "national workshops" that Marx calls for elsewhere.[14] Meanwhile, what are considered useless or socially harmful enterprises will be squeezed out of existence by withholding necessary funds.[15] What is particularly striking about this demand is that it shows the degree of independence to be allowed individual enterprises, whether private or public. If all major decisions were made by some central authority, there would be no need for the state to use credit as a means of control.

"6) Centralization of communication and transport in the hands of the state." Like the previous one, this measure aims at depriving a few capitalists of their power to control the nation's economy, and allows the state to develop its internal communication system on the basis of social need. Another immediate need is that all transportation is made free to the poor.[16] Again, the need to specify that communication and transport are taken over by the state suggests that most fields of endeavor are not.

"7) Extension of factories and instruments of production owned by the state, the bringing in cultivation of waste lands, and the improvement of the soil generally in accordance with a common plan." The involvement of the state in the economy is not concluded when it takes over some enterprises and gains control of others through its monopoly of credit facilities. The state cannot sit on the production laurels of the capitalist economy which preceded it, as imposing as these may be. With the aid of a plan, every effort is made to increase nature's bounty by rapidly increasing and perfecting the means by which it is produced.

"8) Equal liability of all to labor. Establishment of industrial armies, especially for agriculture." The new order brings an end to the parasitic situation existing under capitalism, where the few who don't work are supported by the many who do. Everyone works in communism. Those who don't work don't eat: "Apart from surplus-labor for those who on account of age are not yet, or no longer able to take part in production, all labor to support those who do not work would cease."[17] The freedom to choose one's work is not affected, as some critics assert; just the privilege of choosing not to work is abolished. With everyone working, "productive labor ceases to be a class attribute," allowing Marx to claim that communism "recognizes no class differences because everyone is a worker like everyone else."[18] In calling for the establishment of industrial armies, especially for agriculture, Marx is as concerned with changing the personalities of the people involved as he is with promoting greater economic efficiency.

"9) Combination of agriculture with manufacturing industries; gradual abolition of the distinction between town and country, by a more equable distribution of population over the country." One of the least known of the harmful divisions Marx sees in the human race is between man the "restricted town animal" and man the "restricted country animal."[19] We must remember that, for Marx, peasants are a "class of barbarians," whose way of existence he labels the "idiocy of rural life."[20] People in the country, therefore, need the city and all that it represents in the way of advanced technology and culture, just as people living in the city need the country, its fresh air, inspiring scenery, and toil on the land itself in order to achieve their full stature as human beings. The first stage of communism sees an attempt to create new economic arrangements which will allow men to spend time in cities as well as in the country. The importance Marx attaches to this development can be gathered from his claim that "the abolition of the antagonism between town and country is one of the first conditions of communal life."[21]

Marx believes that the necessary means for healing the split between town and country have already been provided by the preceding mode of production: capitalism, he says, "creates the material conditions for a higher synthesis in the future, namely, the union of agriculture and industry on the basis of the more perfected forms they have each acquired during their temporary separation."[22] We are left to guess what this "higher synthesis" actually looks like, but it appears to involve moving some industries to the country as well as greatly expanding the amount of unencumbered land inside cities for parks, woodland, and garden plots. I suspect, too, that Marx would like to see the number of people living in any one city reduced, and more small and medium size cities set up throughout the countryside, resulting in "a more equable distribution of population over the country" and making possible the establishment of industrial armies for agriculture.

"10) Free education for all children in public schools. Abolition of children's factory labor in its present form. Combination of education with industrial production, etc., etc." In 1848, even elementary education had to be paid for in most countries, so we can easily understand why public education was a major reform.

By "public schools" Marx did not mean "state schools" as this expression is commonly understood. In his "Criticism of the Gotha Program," Marx opposes the Socialist Party's demand for control of "elementary education by the state." He says:

> Defining by a general law the expenditure on the elementary schools, the qualifications of the teaching staff, the branches of instruction, etc., and, as is done in the United States, supervising the fulfillment of these legal specifications by state inspectors, is a very different thing from appointing the state as the educator of the people. Government and church should rather be totally excluded from any influence on the schools.[23]

The people themselves, directly or through social organs still unspecified, will supply the guidelines of their educational system.

In Marx's time, working class children spent the greater part of each day slaving in factories. Clearly, this had to cease immediately. However, Marx did not believe that all this time was better devoted to classroom learning. This, too, would stunt the child's development.[24] Instead he favors an education that "will in the case of every child over a given age, combine productive labor with instruction and gymnastics, not only as one of the methods of adding to the efficiency of production but as the only method of producing fully developed human beings."[25]

III

Not all of the information Marx supplies on the first stage of communism fits neatly into the list of demands found in the *Communist Manifesto:* the state, the conditions and hours of work, the planning for production, and the distribution of what is produced remain to be discussed.

As an instrument of working class rule, the state in this period is labeled, in what has proven to be an unfortunate turn of phrase, the "dictatorship of the proletariat." Hal Draper has demonstrated that "dictatorship" meant something very different to Marx and his contemporaries than it does to most of us.[26] Marx did not use this concept to refer to the extralegal and generally violent rule of one man or a small group of men. Before Hitler and Mussolini, the meaning of "dictatorship" was strongly influenced by its use in ancient Rome, where the constitution provided for the election of a dictator to carry out certain specified tasks for a limited period, generally in times of crisis. It was in opposition to Blanqui's elitist views on the organization of the coming workers' state that Marx first introduced the expression "dictatorship of the proletariat," and by it he meant the democratic rule of the entire working class (including farm laborers), which made up the large majority of the population in all advanced countries.

The dictatorship of the proletariat comes in the wake of the revolution and exists until the onset of full communism. Broadly speaking, its task is to transform the capitalism left behind in all its aspects, material and human, into the full communist society that lies ahead. It functions as a "permanent revolution."[27] As a government, it has a singleness of aim as regards both the past, out of which old enemies are constantly reappearing, and the future, for which it works in a highly systematic way. Marx says:

> "As long as other classes, especially the capitalist class, still exist, as long as the proletariat is still struggling with it (because, with its conquest of governmental power its enemies and the old organization of society have not yet disappeared), it must use coercive means, hence governmental means; it is still a class, and the economic conditions on which the class-struggle and the existence of classes rest, have not yet disappeared and must be removed by force, or transformed, their process of transformation must be speeded up by force.[28]

Where remnants of the old order remain, they are to be removed, the state using all the force necessary for this purpose. Marx's comments elsewhere on the abolition of inheritance, the confiscation of the property of rebels, etc., give an indication of the kind of measures he favored to do away with capitalists as a class. Should individual members of this class prove incorrigible, his statement on the role of the proletarian dictatorship seems to provide a justification for using more extreme means. Marx, however, apparently believed that the economic and social measures introduced by the new regime would be sufficient to transform most capitalists, and that physical violence would only be used against those who resorted to violence themselves.

Most of our details on the workers' government come from Marx's laudatory account of the Paris Commune. The Commune was not a true dictatorship of the proletariat, but it was a close enough approximation to allow us to abstract the general lines, if not the exact configurations, of the coming workers' state. Marx says the "true secret" of the Commune is that "it was essentially a working class government, the product of the struggle of the producing class against the appropriating class, the political form at last discovered under which to work out the economic emancipation of labor."[29]

How, then, was the Commune organized?

The Commune was formed of the municipal councillors, chosen
by universal suffrage in the various wards of the town, responsible and revocable at short terms. . . . The Commune was to be a
working, not a parliamentary body, executive and legislative at the
same time. Instead of continuing to be the agent of the Central
Government, the police was at once stripped of its political
attributes, and turned into the responsible and at all times revocable agent of the Commune. So were the officials of all other
branches of the Administration.[30]

The long arm of popular rule extended into the chambers of
the judiciary, ending what Marx calls their "sham independence." Like the rest of public servants, magistrates and
judges were to be elective, responsible, and revocable."[31]
We also learn that a clear line was drawn between church
and state, and that the army, like the police, was disbanded
and replaced by the armed people.[32]

The organization of the Paris Commune was to serve as a
model not only for the other cities of France, but for small
towns and rural districts as well. Marx says:

The rural communes of every district were to administer their
common affairs by an assembly of delegates in the central town,
and these district assemblies were again to send deputies to the
National Delegation in Paris, each delegate to be at any time revocable and bound by the *mandat imperatif* (formal instructions) of
his constituents. The few but important functions which still
would remain for a central government were not to be suppressed, as has been intentionally misstated, but were to be dis-
charged by Communal, and therefore strictly responsible agents.
. . . While the merely repressive organs of the old government
were to be amputated, its legitimate functions were to be wrested
from an authority usurping pre-eminence over society itself, and
restored to the responsible agents of society. Instead of deciding
once in three or six years which member of the ruling class was
to misrepresent the people in Parliament, universal suffrage was
to serve the people, constituted in Communes, as individual
suffrage serves every other employer in search for the workmen and managers in his business. And it is well known that

companies, like individuals, in matters of real business generally know how to put the right man in the right place, and, if they for once make a mistake, to redress it promptly.[33]

Marx's defense of the Commune's vision of frequent elections for all government functionaries, mandated instructions from their constituents, and the recall reflect his belief that people of all classes recognize, or can be made to recognize, where their best interests lay and to act upon them. But is it really obvious that people usually know or can come to know who will represent their best interests in Parliament? Marx thought it was, and that to open up the channels for popular control, in the absence of capitalist brainwashing techniques, is enough to insure that these interests would be properly represented.

The citizens of the proletarian state, Marx believes, will be able to choose their leaders wisely, but what of the leaders chosen? In marginal notes he wrote into his copy of Bakunin's *State and Anarchism,* Marx gives us his answer to the kind of criticism of Marxism and Russian communism now associated with Milovan Djilas' *New Class.* Far ahead of his time, Bakunin warns that workers, "once they become rulers or representatives of the people, cease to be workers." Next to this comment, Marx writes, "No more than a manufacturer today ceases to be a capitalist when he becomes a member of the municipal council." Bakunin continues, "And from the heights of the State they begin to look down upon the toiling people. From that time on they represent not the people but themselves and their own claims to govern the people. Those who doubt this know precious little about human nature." Besides this, Marx writes, "If Mr. Bakunin were *au courant,* be it only with the position of a manager in a workers' cooperative, he would send all his nightmares about authority to the devil."[34]

Two significant conclusions emerge from this exchange: first, Marx believed people in the government do not have important interests which conflict with those of the class from which they come. Consequently, the elected leaders of the proletarian dictatorship will want to represent the workers correctly. Should the electors make a "mistake," which in this context could only refer to the faulty character of an individual office holder, it will be quickly rectified through the instrument of the recall. Second, to believe that workers elected to government will use their authority to advance personal ends is to have a "nightmare," which in this context I understand to mean a foolish and impossible dream. Marx is asserting, in effect, "The workers are not like that," or, to be more precise, "will not be like that when they come to power." Evidence that this is what has happened in present day communist countries cannot really be used to settle this dispute since the social, economic, and political pre-conditions which Marx thought necessary have never existed in these countries.

So far we have been discussing the dictatorship of the proletariat as if it were the government of a single country. This may be the case immediately after the first revolution, but it is evident that Marx expects this government, within a short space of time, to become worldwide. Capitalism establishes a "universal intercourse" between men, creates in each country the same classes with identical interests and connects them in such a way that no ruling group, whether capitalist or socialist, can succeed on less than a universal basis. Marx states, "Empirically, communism is only possible as the act of the dominant people, 'all at once' or simultaneously."[35] There is no need, therefore, to advise the workers' government on how to deal with the remaining capitalist powers, nor is there any need to provide for a standing army. Marx believed that all the people and means of production currently going to waste in military ventures would become available for useful work. Probably nothing is more responsible for the distortion Marx's vision of communism has undergone in Russia than the fact that the "world revolution" of 1917 succeeded in only a small part of the world.

IV

Marx's description of economic life in the new society is as general and incomplete as his discussion of its political forms. Still, the basic outline of what to expect is there. Inside the factory, an immediate result of the revolution is an improvement in working conditions. Marx attacked the capitalist system for "the absence of all provisions to render the productive process human, agreeable, or at least bearable," and it is clear that the dictatorship of the proletariat gives top priority to correcting this situation.[36] As well as an indictment of existing evils, the description of working conditions in *Capital* can be taken as a roll call of needed reforms. The aim of all action in this field is, first, to make work bearable, then, agreeable, and finally, human.

Hand in hand with the "amelioration" of working conditions goes the shortening of the working day.[37] This is accomplished without any decrease in the total social product. In the only instance where figures are given, it appears that the working day will be cut in half. Marx explains how this is possible: "If everybody must work, if the opposition between those who do work and those who don't disappears . . . and if, moreover, one takes count of the development of the productive forces engendered by capital, society will produce in 6 hours the necessary surplus, even more than now in 12 hours; at the same time everybody will have 6 hours of 'time at his disposition,' the true richness."[38] Another basis for Marx's optimism is seen in his claim that shorter work days will mean greater intensity of labor for the time actually at work.[39]

The very enormity of the cut in hours Marx proposes indicates how great, he believes, is the number of people not working or engaged in useless activity, and also the extent to which capitalism has not taken advantage of its opportunities for technical progress. How else could the revolution cut each worker's day in half while enabling society to produce more than before? In any case, it is clear that Marx's proletariat, unlike Lenin's, does not have to build the industrial base of capitalism before it sets out to build communism. The factories, machines, skills, etc., have been provided in abundance by the preceding era.

Also in the area of production, Marx's views on planning occupy a key position. The immediate aim of all communist planning, he claims, is the satisfaction of "social needs."[40] In deciding how much of any given article to produce, the planners have to strike a balance between social need, available labor-time, and the existing means of production.[41] Although Marx recognizes that demand is elastic, he never doubts that his proletarian planners—whose actual planning mechanisms are never discussed—will make the right equations.

As regards distribution in this period, Marx says, before each individual gets his share of the social product, society must deduct "cover for replacement of the means of production used up. Secondly, additional portion for expansion of production. Thirdly, reserve or insurance funds to provide against accidents, dislocations caused by natural calamities, etc."[42] These inroads into the social product will probably be much larger than their equivalents under capitalism. After society has taken this much out, it must again subtract,

> first, the general costs of adminstration not belonging to production. This part will, from the outset, be very considerably restricted in comparison with present-day society and diminished in proportion as the new society develops. Secondly, that which is intended for the common satisfaction of needs such as schools, health services, etc. From the outset this part grows considerably in comparison with present-day society and it grows in proportion as the new society develops. Thirdly, funds for those unable to work, etc., in short, for what is included under so-called official poor relief today.[43]

Marx's belief that the costs of administration will diminish does not necessarily imply that there will be less government in the short run, though his claim that these costs diminish "in proportion as the new society develops" does imply just this for the long run. The transformation of the professional army into a people's army and the low wages paid to all government functionaries (the example for this was set by the Commune) offer sufficient reasons for the immediate drop in expenses of running a government.[44]

Despite all these inroads into the social product, the portion which goes to each individual is larger than a worker's portion under capitalism.[45] Besides rapid economic growth, this new prosperity is explained by the fact that the outsized shares of the product which went to capitalists, landlords, army officers, bureaucrats, and many industries—now considered wasteful—are divided among everyone. What each person receives directly as his share in the total product, plus the welfare, etc., he gets as a citizen, gives him a material existence that is both secure and comfortable.[46]

So far we have spoken as if all the people living in the first stage of communism receive equal shares of the social product. But this is only true if they work the same amount of time, since the measure guiding distribution for most of this period—it is introduced as soon as it is feasible—is labor-time. Marx claims that each person

> receives back from society—after the deductions have been made— exactly what he gives to it. What he has given to it is his individual quantum of labor. . . . He receives a certificate from society that he has furnished such and such an amount of labor (after deducting his labor for the common funds), and with this certificate he draws from the social stock of means of consumption as much as constitutes the same amount of labor. The same amount of labor which he has given to society in one form he receives back in another.[47]

The Commune's practice of paying everyone in government service, from members of the Commune downwards, the same workmen's wages is declared to be a practical expression of the principle, "equal pay for equal labor-time."[48]

The uses of money are so limited in this period that Marx prefers to speak of "certificates" and "vouchers." Instead of money, what we have are pieces of paper which state how much labor-time one has contributed to the social fund. These simply entitle the individual to draw an equivalent from the fund in the form of consumption goods; means of production and social means of consumption—such as scenic land and trains—are not for sale. As Marx says elsewhere, "These vouchers are not money. They do not circulate."[49] Its circulation between all sectors of the economy has always been a major defining characteristic of money. Such limitations on the power and function of wage payments puts an end to the money system as we know it.

After defending the principle of "equal pay for equal work-time" as marking a notable advance on ideas governing distribution in capitalism, Marx dubs it a "bourgeois limitation." In the first stage of communism, "the right of producers is proportional to the labor they supply; the equality consists in the fact that measurement is made with an equal standard, labor." But he points out,

> one man is superior to another physically or mentally and so supplies more labor in the same time, or can labor for a longer time; and labor, to serve as a measure, must be defined by its duration or intensity, otherwise it ceases to be a standard of measurement. This equal right is an unequal right for unequal labor. It recognizes no class differences, because everyone is only a worker like everyone else; but it tacitly recognizes unequal individual endowment and thus productive capacity as natural privileges. It is, therefore, a right of inequality, in its content, like every right.[50]

The ideal system of distribution, which is foreshadowed in these remarks, would neither punish nor reward people for their personal characteristics.

Marx's picture of life and organization on the first stage of communism is very incomplete. There is no discussion of such obviously important developments as workers' control. We can only guess how much power workers enjoy in their enterprises and through what mechanisms they exercise it on the basis of the democratic processes Marx favors for politics.[51] Cultural institutions and practices are hardly mentioned. Nor is there much said about how conflicts between individuals, between groups, or between the masses and their elected leaders are resolved.

Perhaps more significant is the absence of a list of priorities for the measures favored. Politics is to a large extent the art of arranging priorities, but in what order are Marx's reforms to be tackled? Pointing out that this order is seriously affected by conditions in each country only serves to qualify the question; it doesn't answer it. One would be mistaken, therefore, to view what has been pieced together here as a blueprint of what to do and how to do it. It is but a vision, only one of the ingredients from which blueprints are made—and Marx would not have wanted it otherwise.

V

With the intensification and completion of the various aspects of life and organization associated with the first stage, the second stage of communism gradually makes its appearance. Communism, for we may now drop all qualifying prefixes, is as unlike its immediate predecessor as that society differed from capitalism; yet, the heritage of the first stage is present everywhere. The social ownership of the means of production is a framework structuring all other communist conditions and relations. It is some time since this has been achieved, though it is not so long since it has been completely accepted. Remnants of capitalism no longer exist, either in the mentality of the people or in their conduct, depriving the political dictatorship of the proletariat of its main *raison d'être.*

The wealth which capitalism left and which the first stage of communism multiplied many times over starts communism on its way with a superabundance of all material goods. Wide scale planning has been enormously successful. Technology has developed to a plane where practically anything is possible. Wastelands have been brought under cultivation; a multitude of modern towns have sprung up in the countryside; large cities have been renovated; the communication and transportation systems are as advanced as anything we now have (without actually picturing modern inventions in these fields, and it is approximately this high degree of development which Marx had in mind); factories have become

pleasant places in which to work. At work, where undoubt-
edly the hours have been shortened once again, people have
gotten used to putting in the same amount of time and
receiving equal pay. Elsewhere in society, the education of
the young has proceeded to the point where everyone has
been trained in factories as well as in classrooms.

All such developments are best viewed as constituting the
foundations of communism. What, then, is communism?
Marx's comment on the life and organization that come into
being on these foundations, though even more general and
less systematic than his comments on the first stage, offer a
description of communism that can be summarized in six
main points:

1. The division of labor, as Marx understands it, has come
   to an end, and with it the subjection of individuals to a
   single life task. People now feel the need and have the
   ability to perform many kinds of work.
2. Activity with and for others, at work, in consumption,
   and during free time, has become a prime want, and
   occupies most of the life of every individual.
3. Social ownership has been extended to cover all of nature from the land and the sea to the food each person
   eats and the clothes he wears. Individual ownership, private property in all its guises, has been abolished.
4. Everything with which each person comes into contact,
   which at this time means the entire world, becomes the
   product of his conscious efforts to bend things to his
   own purposes. Instead of submitting to chance as formerly, people, through their knowledge and control
   over natural forces, make their own chance.
5. People's activities are no longer organized by external
   forces, with the exception of productive work where
   such organization still exists, but in the manner of an
   orchestra leader who directs a willing orchestra (the
   example is Marx's). As a part of this, restrictive rules are
   unknown; nor is there any coercion or punishment. The
   state too withers away.
6. The divisions we are accustomed to seeing in the human

species along lines of nation, race, religion, geographical
section (town dweller and country dweller), occupation,
class, and family have all ceased to exist. They are replaced by new and, as yet, unnamed divisions more in
keeping with the character of the people and life of this
period.

The individual's victory over the division of labor is, without a doubt, the central feature of communist society, just
as it is the most difficult one for the uninitiated to grasp.
In previous periods, the necessities of the production process
as well as the social relations of production presented each
person with a single job for life. He was either a worker,
a farmer, a businessman, an intellectual, etc. This was so
even in the first stage of communism, where the amelioration of this condition had already begun. The realities of
one's class position made it impossible, both physically and
from the point of view of attainments, to do work which
lay in the dominion of another class. A striking exception
to this rule is found in the ancient world, and Marx quotes
Lemontey with obvious approval: "We are struck with admi-
ration when we see among the Ancients the same person distinguishing himself to a high degree as a philosopher, poet,
orator, historian, priest, administrator, general of an army.
Our souls are appalled at the sight of so vast a domain. Each
of us plants his hedge and shuts himself up in this enclosure.
I do not know whether by this parcellation the world is enlarged, but I do know that man is belittled."[52]

If such varied activity was possible for a small privileged
class in the ancient world, by the time of capitalism each
class is shut up in its own enclosure; and inside each enclosure parcellation has continued unabated. The final turn of
the screw is applied by "modern industry," where machines
usurp the few human skills that remain, leaving most men
with the minute and highly repetitive operations involved in
machine minding. In this situation, leisure activities can only
be of the kind that come naturally, men having neither the
time nor the opportunity to acquire special talents and tastes.

Life in communism is at the opposite extreme from what

exists in capitalism. In the new society, people do many kinds of work where their ancestors used to do one. Both manual and intellectual activity form a part of every working day, for, according to Marx, "the antithesis between mental and physical labor has vanished."[53] Humankind is no longer divided into sheep and goats, and given their work tasks accordingly. The individual is declared rich in communism because he needs "the totality of human life activities."[54] And he enjoys them, to a large extent, just because they are so varied.

But the break with the parcellation of the past is more radical still. For in the new society, there are no more weavers, metal workers, coal miners, plumbers, farmers, factory managers, engineers, or professors. These labels are used to categorize people who are tied down to a particular occupation for life. In communism, the tie is unknotted, and each person takes part, at one time or another, in many if not most of these activities. Perhaps Marx's best known statement on this subject is his claim that

> in communist society, where nobody has one exclusive sphere of activity but each can become accomplished in any branch he wishes, society regulates the general production and thus makes it possible for me to do one thing today another tomorrow, to hunt in the morning, fish in the afternoon, rear cattle in the evening, criticize after dinner, just as I have a mind, without ever becoming hunter, fisherman, shepherd or critic.[55]

These are unfortunate examples to show how diversified man's endeavors become, for they have led some to believe that life in communism is all play and no work—anyway, no factory work. But factory work, in the new social form which it takes in this period, is an activity to which all people devote some time. It is something which everybody, without exception, wants to do. [56]

Besides contributing to production, each individual also participates in cultural and scientific life, and not just as a consumer of other people's products but as a creator. We have met communist man as worker, farmer, hunter, and critic, and Marx now introduces us to the same person as artist: "The exclusive concentration of artistic talent in some individuals and its suppression in the grand mass which springs from this, is a consequence of the division of labor. . . . In a communist society, there are no painters, but men who among other things do painting."[57] Being a painter is to be subjected to the division of labor as much as if one only did weaving. Every person in communist society is relieved of the burden of narrowness which plagued his ancestors, weavers and painters alike, and given the opportunity to express himself in all possible ways.

What applies to painting also applies to science. The scientist, as someone who devotes his entire working life to science, is replaced in this period by the whole citizenry, who spend part of their time doing theoretical as well as practical scientific work. People in communism relate to other activities ranging from athletics to courting to musing on one's own in the same way.

Marx not only ascribes a world of activities to the communist man, but believes he will be very proficient in their performance. To achieve this is the aim of communist education.[58] At the same time, Marx recognizes that not all people will be equally good in everything they try. As regards painting, for example, he admits that only a few will rise to the level of Raphael. On the other hand, the quality of other people's work will be extremely high; and he maintains, all paintings will be original.[59] By "original," I take him to mean that each person's creative efforts will be a true expression of his unique qualities. Marx would probably be willing to make a similar distinction between average and exceptional ability in science, farming, material production, etc., always with the proviso that those who lag behind are still extraordinarily good.

Even in communism, people do not have the time to become equally skilled in all tasks. There is just too much to do. Hence, those who spend more time learning surgery will be better surgeons in any social system. Furthermore, men will always possess different intellectual and physical capacities.[60] Marx does not dismiss heredity, though the nature of its effect is never revealed to us beyond the generalities of more and better. Yet, despite these admissions, the least gifted men in communism are spoken of as if they are more accomplished than Lemontey's heroes, and do each of their tasks with a high degree of skill.

To those who argue that skill is invariably a function of specialization, Marx would probably reply that, insofar as specialization involves learning a body of data and technique, communist people are specialists in many tasks. The exclusive quality which we associate with specialization is viewed as a social side effect that is destined to disappear. In the past, outstanding contributions to civilization were often the work of one-sided "geniuses," who—compared to their no-sided contemporaries—realized at least some of their potential. The difference is that the many-sided men living in communism are able to learn a great variety of skills quickly, and, hence, to develop a wide range of powers. Everything in their society is bent to facilitate these efforts, and the character of each individual—itself the product of communist conditions—insures that he is able to make the most of his opportunities.[61]

Another major characteristic of the communist society is the high degree of cooperation and mutual concern which is discernible in most human activities. One indication of this development is simply the increase in the number of things people do in common. Reference has already been made to the "industrial armies" which do the work formerly done by peasants on their own plots. Beyond this, Marx claims, "communal activity and communal consumption—that is, activity and consumption which are manifested and directly confirmed in real association with other men—will occur wherever such a direct expression of sociality stems from the true character of the activity's content and is adequate to the nature of consumption."[62]

We are not told which activities have a "character" that requires they be done communally. Nor do we learn what types of consumption have a "nature" that requires communal consumption. Consequently, we do not really know how far Marx would extend his principle in practice. All we can be certain of is that cooperation will cover far more than it does today. Marx speaks, for example, of new "social organs" coming into existence which are the institutional forms of new social activities as well as the new forms adapted for old ones.[63]

Of greater significance than the spread of cooperation is the fact that it is qualitatively superior to what goes by the same name in earlier periods. Marx believed that production is social in any society since it is always carried on inside some relationship with other people. However, the cooperation involved varies from tenuous, unconscious, and forced, at one extreme, to close, conscious, and free, at the other. In communism, interdependence becomes the recognized means to transform the limitations set by what was until now an unrecognized interdependence.

Because people at this time are "brought into practical connection with the material and intellectual production of the whole world," interdependence is world wide and grasped as such.[64] These relations lead each individual to become conscious of humanity as part of himself, which is to say of himself as a "social being."[65] This is not only a matter of considering social interdependence as a facet of one's own existence, but of thinking (and, therefore, treating) the needs of others as one's own, experiencing happiness when they are happy and sadness when they are sad, and believing that what one controls or does is equally theirs and their doing, and vice versa. Perhaps nothing in the communist society helps explain the extraordinary cooperation which characterizes this period as much as the individual's new conception of himself, which, in turn, could only emerge full blown as a product of such cooperation.[66]

In discussing the first stage of communism, we saw that the satisfaction of social needs had become the accepted goal of material production. By full communism, this goal has sunk into the consciousness of each individual, determining how he views all the products of his work. Besides the sense of devotedness which comes from feeling oneself part of a productive unit (and the productive unit a part of oneself), each person gives his best because he is aware of the needs of those who use his products (and because he conceives of these needs as his own). He realizes that the better he does the more satisfaction he gives. [67] Communist man's concern for his fellows as coproducers is matched by his concern for them as consumers of what he has helped to produce.

This desire to please is not associated with any sense of duty, but with the satisfaction one gets at this time in helping others. Assuming the role of communist man, Marx proclaims, "in your joy or in your use of my product, I would have the direct joy from my good conscience of having, by my work, satisfied a human need . . . and consequently, of having procured to the need of another human being his corresponding object." [68] We can approximate what takes place here if we view each person as loving his fellows such that he can get pleasure from the pleasure they derive from his efforts. This should not be so hard to conceive when we think of how close friends and relatives often get pleasure from the happiness they give each other. Marx is universalizing this emotion, much enriched, to the point where each person is able to feel it for everyone whom his actions affect, which in communism is the whole of society. Everywhere the individual recognizes and experiences the other as the "complement" of his own "nature" and as a "necessary part" of his own "being." [69] Aside from considerations of getting something done, people at this time also engage in communal activities for the sheer pleasure of being with others. Human togetherness has become its own justification. [70]

A third characteristic distinctive of the communist society is the replacement of private property by social ownership in personal as well as public effects. [71] Communism is spoken of in one place as "the positive transcendence of private property." [72] We have already seen the role social ownership of the means of production plays in the first stage of communism in enabling wide scale planning, promoting equality, and securing better working conditions. Small businesses, however, still existed at least at the beginning of the first stage, and articles subject to direct consumption were still owned as private property. Most people attached great value to the particular objects they used because these were not easy to replace, and, in any case, cost money (labor vouchers) which could be spent on something else. Under such conditions, cooperation did not extend to sharing all that one had with others, and the possessive attitude so prevalent today still had to be reckoned with, though probably less among the proletariat who had fewer material possessions to begin with than among the small holding peasants and the remnants of the bourgeoisie.

Private property, by its very nature, secures the owner special rights over and against all nonowners. It is essentially a negative notion, an assertion, backed by the full coercive force of society, that one man may exclude others from using or benefiting from whatever it is he owns if he so desires. It assumes the possibility—indeed, the inevitability—of a clash between what he wants to do with his objects and what others want to do with them. What happens, then, to the notion of private property in a society where no one ever claims a right to the things he is using, wearing, eating, or living in, where instead of refusing to share with others he is only too happy to give them what they want, where—if you like—all claims to use are considered equally legitimate? This is the situation in communism: the clash of competing interests has disappeared and with it the need to claim rights of any sort.

We have just seen how aware each communist person is of what effect his actions have on others and how concerned he is with their obtaining satisfaction, both because his own personal needs require it and because he has conceptualized himself as a social being of which they are integral parts. It is this which allows him to say "the senses and enjoyment of other men have become my own appropriation."[73] Consequently, if one person has something another wants, his first reaction is to give it to him. Of private property in land, Marx says, "From the stand-point of a higher economic form of society, private ownership of the globe by single individuals will appear quite as absurd as private ownership of one man by another."[74] In full communism, with human relationships as I have depicted them, private ownership of anything will appear equally ridiculous. It should be clear that it is never a matter of people depriving themselves for the sake of others. Consumption for all citizens is that which "the full development of the individual requires."[75] The community stores are replete with everything a communist person could possibly want. "To each according to his need" is the promise communist society makes to all of its members.[76]

Private property has always been based, in a fundamental sense, on the existence of material scarcity. This applies to the dictatorship of the proletariat as well as to earlier periods. What one man or a few had could not be acquired by the many, because there simply was not enough to go around. But, when supply is so plentiful that everyone can have as much of anything as he wants just for the asking, the social relationships that rest on existing scarcity are turned upside down. Only on this foundation can people view whatever they happen to be using at the moment as social objects, as products made by everyone for everyone. There is no longer "mine," "yours," "his," and "hers," but only "ours."

VI

Another unique attribute of communist society is the masterly control which human beings exercise over all the forces and objects of nature. In communism, Marx declares, the task "is to put in place of the supremacy of exterior conditions and of chance over the individuals, the supremacy of the individuals over chance and objective conditions."[77] This is also referred to as "the casting off of all natural limitations."[78] These are limitations placed on people's activities by the sum of the nonhuman circumstances in which they find themselves, and what formerly, through ignorance, was labeled "natural law."

For Marx, the "laws of nature" which are said to govern us are "founded on the want of knowledge of those whose action is the subject to it."[79] There is no want of knowledge about nature in the new society. People understand their total environment, how it functions, and what its possibilities are. Implicit in Marx's view is the belief that when communist people fully comprehend nature they will not desire anything which stands outside their effective reach. This belief, in turn, is based on his conception of how far people's reach actually extends in communism and accompanying assumptions regarding the creative potential of their cooperation. Marx is saying, in effect, that much of what people today want to do, but cannot, will be done under the ideal conditions of communism, that what remains are things which the extraordinary people of this time will not want to do, and, most important, that what they will want to do which we do not (we caught a glimpse of what this might be in presenting the material prerequisites of communism) they will easily accomplish.

Yet, so complete is their grasp of the interconnected parts which constitute communist reality that Marx foresees natural science and human science will become one.[80] It is in this sense too that he later says man "becomes able to understand his own history as a process, and to conceive of nature (involving also practical control over it) as his own real body."[81] What is involved here is becoming conscious of the internal relations between what are today called "natural" and "social" worlds, and treating the hitherto separate halves as a single totality. In learning about either society or nature, the individual will recognize that he is learning about both.

Communist people cannot change the climate (or can they?), but they can take all its effects into consideration and make their broader plans accordingly. As for the rest, Marx seems to believe that a united and cooperating mankind can dominate nature directly, and his conception of the productive potential of industry seems closer to the reality we expect for tomorrow than the one we have today. We are told that "the reality which communism is creating is precisely the real basis for rendering it impossible that anything exist independently of individuals, in so far as things are only a product of the preceding intercourse of individuals themselves."[82]

As for those objects and processes not already a part of human intercourse, Marx declares, man, "for the first time, consciously treats all natural premises as the creatures of men, strips them of their natural character and subjugates them to the power of individuals united."[83] Thus, the whole world is regarded through the eyes of a creator; everything people come into contact with is altered to suit their wide-ranging purposes; former barriers have been transformed into freeways; nothing is allowed to block their fulfillment, and nothing which can contribute to it is permitted to remain neutral. Viewing people's ties with nature as logically internal relations over which each person in conjunction with his fellows has now gained conscious mastery, Marx can claim that in communism "nature becomes man."[84]

Marx does not supply us with a map of communist topography, so we are left with the notion that physical changes are enormous without knowing in much detail what they are. We have already come across some of them, such as the spatial reorganization of town and countryside. Probably nothing shows the extent to which Marx foresaw human domination over nature better, however, than his comment that language will "submit to the perfect control of individuals."[85] I interpret this to mean that one language will replace the thousands now in existence (whatever limited cultural role many languages may continue to play), and that it will be specially adapted to permit clear expression of the extraordinary experiences, understanding, and feelings of the people of this time.

The key to the individual's newly arrived at domination over nature lies in the peculiar quality of communist cooperation. Marx labels cooperation in any historical period a "productive force," which is a way of saying that the form of social interaction as such is partly responsible for the quantity and quality of its products.[86]

The difference is that in communism, where work in common is the rule and everyone gives himself fully to all his tasks, cooperation is a productive force of practically limitless potential. According to Marx, "It is just this combination of individuals (assuming the advanced stage of modern productive forces, of course) which puts the conditions of the free development and movement of individuals under their control."[87]

VII

A fifth striking feature of communism is the absence of external rules and, with it, of all forms of coercion and discipline. Aside from work in factories and on farms, none of the activities people engage in at this time are organized; that is to say, there is nothing they must do and no predetermined manner or time restrictions which they must follow in doing it. On the other hand, coordination is the minimal demand which social production per se makes on all its participants. Hence, some organization, headed by someone whose job it is to coordinate productive tasks, is required of every society. According to Marx, "in all kinds of work where there is cooperation of many individuals, the connection and the unity of the process are necessarily represented in a will which commands and in functions which, as for the leader of an orchestra, are not concerned with partial efforts, but the collective activity. It is there a productive work which must be accomplished in any mode of combined production." He calls this "the work of general supervision and of direction."[88]

However, even in production, the organization which Marx foresees in communism is a far cry from what exists today. Though factories and farms still possess managers, their duties are simply to coordinate the efforts of those who work under them; they act as leaders of an orchestra. Since people in communism are frequently changing jobs, we can assume that at one time or another almost everyone will serve as a manager. The orchestra which is being directed is always willing and enthusiastic, since its goals and those of the manager are the same, viz., to produce articles which satisfy social needs, and to produce all that is required, of the best quality, in the shortest possible time, and with the least amount of waste. In capitalism, workers do as little and as shoddy a job as they can get away with and their bosses are constantly after them to work even more and harder than they could if they were really trying. In communism, laziness, which Marx views as a historically conditioned phenomenon, would die a natural death.[89] "From each according to his ability" is a promise that no one at this time would think of breaking.[90]

In production where each individual works to the best of his ability, factory discipline with all its paraphernalia of fines, dismissals, threats, etc., has become obsolete. Marx claims such discipline "will become superfluous under a social system in which the laboreres work for their own account, as it has already become practically superfluous in piece-work."[91] Whenever workers recognize that by exerting themselves they can increase their share of the product, they do not have to be coerced to work. In communism, each worker-musician does his best to keep time with the rest of the orchestra.

What have we learned about work in communism? Without coercion and full of mutual concern, in pleasant surroundings and for relatively short periods each day (week?), people use the socially owned means of production to control and transform nature to satisfy human needs. Frequently changing tasks, they find both joy and fulfillment in their cooperation and its momentous achievements. Unlike Fourier, however, who compares work in communism to play, Marx says it will be earnest and intense effort as befits any truly creative activity.[92] Still—in an-oft quoted phrase— Marx refers to production in communism as the "realm of necessity" and contrasts it with the "realm of freedom," or nonwork activity, where the "development of human energy . . . is an end in itself."[93] The fact is that whether communist people want to or not they have to do some work just in order to live; that they invariably want to is beside the point.

If this qualification places work in the *realm* of necessity, however, it doesn't follow that work is an unfree activity. In his most forthright statement on this subject, Marx calls man's freedom "the positive power to assert his true individuality."[94]   Given the character of work in communism, including the degree of control over nature exercised in work, it is the equal of any other activity in bringing out and developing the unique potential in each human being.   Consequently, Marx can speak of work in this period as the "activity of real freedom."[95]

If people in communism are so cooperative that the only productive organization is that minimum required by economic efficiency, then we may expect that even this minimum will disappear in the nonwork areas of life.   In one listing, we learn that soldiers, policemen, hangmen, legislators, and judges are equally unnecessary "under proper conditions of society."[96]   Without any need for coercion, the institutionalized means by which it is exercised can be eliminated.[97]   This victory over external authority is a victory of the accusers as well as of the accused, for as Marx says, "punishment, coercion is contrary to human conduct."[98]

With the sole exception of production, all forms of organization adopted in the dictatorship of the proletariat serve in the role of Wittgenstein's ladder for communist man; they enable him to climb into communism, only to be discarded when he gets there.   Restrictive rules, coercion of all kinds, become worse than nuisances—they constitute actual obstructions—in a society which knows no clash of basic interests.

Perfect success is too much to ask from the full time job Marx gives each communist man of being his brother's keeper.   Consequently, whenever an individual fails in one of the tasks he has set himself or, through carelessness—we cannot conceive of any more wicked motive operating on him—breaks a norm or causes harm to others, he himself administers the punishment. Marx declares that,

> under human conditions, punishment will really be nothing but the sentence passed by the culprit on himself. There will be no

attempt to persuade him that violence from without, exerted
on him by others, is violence on himself by himself. On the
contrary, he will see in other men his natural saviours from the
sentence which he has pronounced on himself; in other words the
relation will be reversed.[99]

Given the social-mindedness referred to earlier, any significant lapse in a person's cooperative behavior will provoke
feelings of guilt. Guilt is a burden that can only be removed
by others. In communism, society's role has changed from
punishing wrongdoers to reassuring and soothing them to
help relieve their self-inflicted anguish.

We should not be surprised to learn that in these conditions
there is no place for a state. Simply put, the state withers
away because there is nothing further for it to do. The main
work of the dictatorship of the proletariat was to destroy all
remnants of capitalism and to construct the foundations for
full communism. Laws, organization, discipline, coercion,
etc., were all necessary to accomplish these ends. But now
communism is the reality, and capitalism is history. Marx
says, "When, in the course of development, class distinctions
have disappeared, and all production has been concentrated
in the hands of associated individuals, the public power will
lose its political character. Political power, properly so called,
is merely the organized power of one class for oppressing
another."[100] What does a state without a "political character"
look like? Marx rephrases this question to read, "What social
functions will remain in existence there that are analogous to
present functions of the state?"[101] Though he never gives a
full answer, it is clear what his answer would be.

The three main functions of any state are legislation, ajudi-
cation, and administration. Of legislation, Marx says, in
communism all forms of parliamentarism will be "ranged
under the category of nuisances."[102] Legislatures are political expressions of the principle of majority rule which, in
turn, is based on the assumption that on important matters
people's opinions are bound to clash. They are battlefields of
the class struggle, battlefields on which the ruling economic

class, obtaining its majority by means fair and foul, legislates repeated defeats for the opposition. But the people of communism are agreed on all subjects which could possibly come before a parliament. Where interests merge and decisions are unanimous it is not necessary to go through all the formality of counting hands. Furthermore, all really major decisions, those bearing on the structure of communism itself, have already been taken by this time. People have what they want, that is, communism, and there is nothing for a legislature, whose main function is to make changes, to change.

The judicial arm of government, too, is based on an assumption of necessary conflict between people. From the quasi-sanctification of a raised bench, the ruling class, in the person of some of its more pompous representatives, renders biased interpretations of one-sided laws. But if this conflict doesn't exist . . . ? A typical case which comes before courts everywhere is a suit for injuries. In the communist society, a person who is harmed by another suffers no economic disadvantages because of it (he continues to take from the social stock of goods whatever he needs); moreover, he knows that the party who struck the blow did not do it on purpose, and that the pain of a guilty conscience is as great or greater than the pain coming from the injury. Rather than insisting on revenge or compensation, our victim would probably join with coworkers and neighbors to ease the guilt of the person who injured him. All "claims for damages" will be dispensed with in this way, by the people concerned directly. The other cases which come before our courts today, those involving murder, robbery, kidnapping, forgery, etc., simply do not exist. They have been made either impossible, since everything people want is free, and legal papers which secure special rights and powers don't exist, or unnecessary, since there is nothing people want that requires such antisocial measures. What, then, is the need for courts?

The case of the administration is a bit more complicated. One main function of the administrative branch of government is to enforce the laws. In communist society, where there are no laws and where social norms are accepted and heeded by all, this function no longer exists. But another task remains which is comparable to the coordination provided by factory managers. In the area of production, communist society as a whole, like its individual enterprises, will require the general supervision of managers. Duplication as well as gaps in production and services have to be prevented. Coordinating efforts, therefore, will be needed at all the major crossroads of social life, wherever, in fact, a traffic director is useful in helping people to get where they want to go.

Some might argue that this coordinating function conceals acts of legislation and adjudication, and that administrators are the new lawgivers and judges of this period, but communism is unique in having administrators and administered who are striving to achieve the same ends. Their mutual trust and concern with one another are likewise complete. Consequently, the minor alterations and judgements required of any administration are accepted as expressions of a common will. Recall, too, that each individual has come to conceive of his fellows as parts of himself, as extensions of his nature as a social being, so even when he is not directly involved in administration he feels himself involved through his relations with those who are. Furthermore, since the activity of coordinating social life at its various levels is something everyone will undertake at some time or another, there is no special strata of administrators. To describe this state of affairs in terms of "legislature," "laws," "courts," etc., is extremely misleading. This work of administration, more properly of coordination, is the only function in communism which is analogous to the duties of a modern state.

Distributing these administrative tasks takes place through an election which Marx describes as a "business matter." Since everyone agrees on matters of policy, elections are probably uncontested. In any case, victory does not "result in any domination." We are assured that an election in communism has "none of its present political character." Elections are merely a way of passing administrative jobs around to people who are more or less equally equipped to carry them out. In these conditions, Marx is able to claim that "the whole people will govern; there will be no one to be governed."[103] Marx, however, prefers to play down the role of coordinating authority in the new society, emphasizing instead the power which comes through direct cooperation.

Could a complex industrial society be run in this manner? Marx believed it could not be run as effectively in any other. After all, many of the worst administrative complexities are byproducts of present social organization and its accompanying attitudes. Most records, for example, are only kept to secure a limited number of people—the young, the old, the sick, veterans, etc.—rights which in communism are universal (or, as Marx would prefer, which have disappeared for everyone because they are no longer necessary for anyone). The extensive red tape bureaucracies for which modern day "socialist" countries are noted do not offer any indication of what to expect when the special conditions Marx lays down for communism have been fulfilled. Likewise, a great deal of administrative calculation, in government as elsewhere, is devoted to getting people to obey rules they don't like by deciding what incentives to offer and how to punish slackers. Manipulations connected with improving the position of privileged segments of the ruling class or trying to harmonize competing social interests are other components of existing complexity. With new aims and standards, and, above all, new communist people, most of what makes social administration an unfathomable labyrinth will disappear. Simple cooperation within each functional social unit together with single purpose coordination between them provides communism as an advanced industrial society with all the "administration" it requires.

VIII

Sixth and last, communist society is also unique in the kind of human groups it has and does not have. The mankind we know is divided into various nations, races, religions, geographical sections (town dweller or country dweller), classes, occupations, and families. No doubt, for many people a world where these distinctions cannot be made is inconceivable. Yet, this is just the situation Marx introduces us to in communism where, first of all, our globe is no longer divided into countries.[104] An approach to grasping what Marx means is to imagine the whole world as one nation. One should recognize, however, that the term "nation" has been imported from the vocabulary of another time. The world as a nation performs none of the functions associated with the nations of old. We have just seen how the state has withered away; there is no world parliament, world court, or world army, and—aside from some world managers to coordinate production on this macrocosmic scale—there is no world executive.

Both as a producer and as a consumer, the individual is profoundly affected by the disappearance of the state. Marx tells us that in their artistic endeavors—and everyone at this time engages in some kind of artistry—communist people are no longer subjected to national limitations.[105] No longer bound by the experience, tastes, and tools of his locality, each person is able to express his emotions and thoughts in a universal manner. If art can free itself of the limiting effect of customs, so can material production and indeed everything else people do once the constraints of nationhood and nationalism are removed. I have already noted Marx's belief that everyone will eventually speak a single language.[106] The existence of such a language does not mean that lesser local languages and the distinctive cultures which accompany them will all disappear. Latin and Latin culture have enriched the lives of millions long after the decline of the Roman empire, and I expect the same fate awaits other tongues and traditions which are now widespread.

The cosmopolitanism of man as producer is matched by his new cosmopolitanism as consumer. People are able to use and fully appreciate all manner of products. Of this period, Marx says, "Only then will the separate individuals be liberated from the various national and local barriers, be brought into practical connection with the material and intellectual production of the whole world and be put in a position to acquire the capacity to enjoy this all-sided production of the whole earth [the creations of man]."[107]

Religious divisions between men have also ceased to exist in communism with the demise of all mystical beliefs. Superstition has given way to science, and individual fear and weakness to the power of the community. What Marx calls "the witchery of religion" is no more.[108] Communist people are not atheists; this is a term Marx avoids because of its suggestion of being antireligion. The truth is that religion has stopped being a matter of concern. People are neither for nor against it; they are disinterested. As with the state, religion simply withers away as its functions disappear.

The distinction between city-bred and country-bred people also falls by the wayside in communism where the whole countryside is spotted with cities and cities are equally invaded by the countryside.[109] Divisions between people on the basis of class were practically nonexistent in the first stage of communism, where everyone was already a worker. In one place, Marx goes so far as to claim that with everyone engaged in productive work classes cease to exist.[110] Yet, we also know that a major task of the dictatorship of the proletariat is to control and convert remnants of the capitalist class, so not every "worker" in this transition period is an equal member of the proletariat.[111] Marx uses several criteria to assess class membership, and it is simply that the dictatorship of the proletariat is classless in some senses and not in others.[112] By full communism, all of Marx's criteria for a classless society have been met.

As for setting people apart because of their occupations, this went out with permanent occupations. Each person in communism engages in a variety of productive tasks. Probably the least known of Marx's projections for communism has to do with the end of racial divisions. Marx did not enjoy floundering so deeply in the unknown; nevertheless, his single expression of opinion on this subject is very forthright. While discussing the effect of environment, Marx says:

The capacity for development of infants depends on the development of parents and all the mutilations of individuals, which are
an historical product of ancient social conditions, are equally
capable of being historically avoided. Even the natural diversity
of species, as for example the differences of race, etc. . . . are and
must be checked historically.[113]

Marx is not just referring to a few racial characteristics; his
words are "the differences of race." No doubt, he saw some
differences as easier to change than others, but if so, this is
nowhere stated. When we consider the quality of the cooperation which exists between all people in communism and
their ready access to one another, it is not surprising that
Marx envisioned a time—perhaps thousands of years hence—
when all the world's races have blended into one.

If the least known of Marx's projections for communism
is the end of racial divisions, probably the best known—and
maybe for that reason the most distorted—is the abolition of
the family. Marx spoke of the "earthly family" being destroyed "both in theory and in practise" in communism.[114]
Some people have taken this to mean the end of all intimate
relationships, free love, forced separation from children, and
many other "immoralities," each more gross than the one
before. Marx is guilty of none of these sins. To begin with,
the form of the family that he claims will disappear is the
bourgeois family. According to him, this is a form based on
capital and private gain, in which economic advantage is the
main reason for entering marriage, in which the male has
practically all the rights, in which parents have almost total
power over their children, and in which the stifling closeness
between members of the family excludes most kinds of inti-
macy with other people.[115] The task of abolishing this form
of the family had been begun by the bourgeoisie themselves
when they forced conditions of life upon their workers which
made it impossible for them to spend much time with their
wives and children, and destroyed all privacy when they were
together. It is in this sense that Marx maintains the family
had practically ceased to exist among the proletariat.[116]

The communist alternative to the family is never stated very clearly, but it can be pieced together from Marx's scattered comments on this subject. Its main features appear to be group living, monogamous sexual relationships, and the communal raising of children. The group living aspect is apparent from Marx's contrast of the family with what he calls a "communal domestic economy."[117] All the advances of modern science are used to make living together as comfortable and harmonious as possible. Whether people eat in communal dining rooms, sleep in the same building, share household tasks, etc., are not disclosed, though I suspect this is the kind of thing Marx had in mind.

A great deal of the abuse leveled against communism has been directed at what is really a phantom of the bourgeois imagination. The abolition of the family and free love, that is indiscriminate sexual activity by both sexes, are almost always joined together in the minds of those who criticize communism. Marx, however, opposes sexual promiscuity (at least for adults) both for the society in which he lives and for communism. His hostility to the sexual antics of the bourgeoisie and the sarcasm with which he treats charges of the same in communism are clear evidence of this.[118] He also attacks the school he calls "crude communism" for having as one of its goals "the community of women."[119] Sex in his ideal society is always associated with love, and love of this kind appears to be an exclusive if sometimes temporary relationship between one man and one woman. The universal love which was alluded to in our discussion of cooperation in communism does not include engaging indiscriminately in the sexual act, for Marx acknowledges there will continue to be something like unrequited love and calls it a misfortune.[120]

To grasp Marx's views on this subject, it is necessary to see that he is wholly on the side of love and lovers, that he demands a full equality for both partners, and that he views sexual love in communism as the highest expression of the new kind of relationship which exists between all people in this period. In *The Holy Family,* that extended review of Eugene Sue's novel *Mysteries of Paris,* Marx sides time and time again with the most sensual characters, with those who can and want to love.[121] And in the *Economic and Philosophic Manuscripts of 1844* we learn that women have become men's equals in love as in all else, and that the type of mutual consideration which characterizes sexual love in communism has become the measure of perfection for all contacts with other people.[122]

The communal raising of children is never mentioned explicitly, but can be deduced from other aspects of communist life which seem to require it. For Marx, aside from minor differences due to heredity, a child's development is determined by his environment, an important part of which is the parental home. In capitalism, parents have considerable control over their children's health, education, work, marriage, etc., but, given the parent's own problems and limitations, this power is seldom used wisely. In communism, parents will no longer exercise a destructive influence on their children. This does not mean that they will be forcibly separated from their young. Given communist sociality, without the pervading selfishness and emotional insecurity which characterize current parent-child relations, communist parents will want a community no less perfect for their children than they construct for themselves.

Not only children, of course, but adults as well require special conditions to realize their full human potential. We have already seen the importance Marx attaches to free time. Though he never deals with the drain children are on their parents, particularly on mothers, he surely was aware of it. Already living in the "communal domestic economy," the arrangement which seems best suited to permit the self-realization of young and old alike is some kind of communal raising of children. Parents and children simply spend as much time together and apart as their respective development requires. Unlike today, however, the time together is devoted to activities which bring mutual pleasure and growth, for this interaction is no longer rooted in necessary work and customary duties, but in the same desire to satisfy common needs which characerizes all social contact in the communist society.[123]

It should be clear by now that Marx is far more precise about the social and other divisions which will disappear in communism than about what will replace them. Nations, religions, geographical sections, classes, occupations, races, and families are to disappear, but what new social categories will emerge? It is important that any attempt to answer specify that Marx viewed all such divisions as barriers to the direct contact between people and, therefore too, to the fulfillment of human potential in so far as it requires this contact. Erasing social lines per se, then, is a major task of the dictatorship of the proletariat, and fusion of the once separate and distinct social categories is one of the surest signs that communism has arrived.

However, even communism contains boundary lines of a sort which allow some distinctions between people to be made. From what has been said, it would appear that these new subdivisions, like the social organs they contain, are consciously designed functional units which merely express the most efficient and humane ways of getting things done. The factory, the communal domestic economy, and the industrial army for agriculture are examples of the functional units into which communist society is divided. With people changing jobs as often as they do, however, it is unlikely that a person will carry one work place label for very long. I suspect that distinctions based on membership in communal domestic economies are of a more durable nature, since home groups are likely to be more permanent than work groups.

These boundary lines in communist society are never barriers to direct human contact. For though they aid us in making passing distinctions between individuals, they do not really substitute for our understanding of them as people, as the corresponding attributes do in an earlier period. The difference is that everyone at this time possesses or could easily acquire the credentials for membership in any group. Thus, when discussing communism, Marx dismisses its particular associations and directs all his remarks to the species, to human beings who are forever dividing and re-dividing society in pursuit of human goals.[124]

IX

Our reconstruction of communism is now complete, or as complete as Marx's diverse comments permit. As a way of life, communism develops in people extraordinary qualities which are themselves necessary for this way of life to operate. What are these qualities? On the basis of the foregoing account we can say that the citizen of the future is someone who is highly and consistently cooperative, who conceives of all objects in terms of "ours," who shares with his fellow men a masterful control over the forces of nature, who regulates his activities without the help of externally imposed rules, and who is indistinguishable from his fellows when viewed from the perspective of existing social divisions. He (she) is, in short, a brilliant, highly rational and socialized, humane, and successful creator. In a terminology preferred by a younger Marx, this is the accomplished figure who "brings his species powers out of himself" and "grasps the human nature of need," the same who "appropriates his total essence . . . as a whole man."[125]

Each part of this description of people in communism can serve as the full account once its relations with the whole are recognized. An individual could only engage successfully in so many activities if he cooperates with his fellows at every turn, treats all material objects as belonging to the group, enjoys the requisite power over nature, etc. In the same way, he can only exercise communist sociality if he is able to do a variety of tasks with the ease of an expert, treat objects as "ours," and the rest. Just as no aspect of communist life can arise independently, none of the qualities ascribed to communist people can emerge alone. As internally related parts of an organic whole, each assumes and is based on the presence of all. Marx's best known descriptions of communism—that it is a classless society, a time when the division of labor has disappeared, and when private property has been abolished—are all to be viewed in this light.[126] Rather than partial, one-sided alternatives, these descriptions of communism (including each other as necessary conditions and/or results) are equally complete, the only difference being one of focus and emphasis within the totality.

The qualities and life Marx ascribes to the people of communism represent a complete victory over the alienation that has characterized humanity's existence throughout class society, reaching its culmination in the relations between workers and capitalists in modern capitalism. At the core of alienation is the separation of the individual from the conditions of human existence, chiefly his activities (particularly production), their real and potential products, and other people. As a result of class divisions and accompanying antagonisms, people have lost control over the objective manifestations of their humanity, grossly misunderstanding them in the process, coming eventually to service the "needs" of their own creations. Viewing whatever people do and use to satisfy their needs and realize their powers as elements of human nature, the progressive dismemberment of human nature (alienation) becomes identical with the stunting and distortion of potential in each real individual. The bringing together or reunification on a higher technological plane of the elements of human nature that earlier societies had torn asunder begins with the revolution, gains momentum in the dictatorship of the proletariat, and is only completed in full communism.

As opposites, alienation and communism serve as necessary points of reference for each other. A theoretically adequate description of communism, therefore, would have to include an extended account of alienation. I have offered such an account elsewhere.[127] In the present essay, I have been content to sacrifice some theoretical adequacy to the demands of a simpler, more coherent vision.

The question that remains is how to evaluate Marx's vision of communism. Experience is not a relevant criterion, though the history of the species should make us sensitive to the enormous flexibility of human needs and powers. It is no use to say (though people continue to say it) that such a society has never existed and that the people Marx depicts have never lived. The communist society is the ultimate achievement of a long series of developments which begin with the socialist appropriation of the capitalist mode of production. Its distinctive characteristics evolve gradually out of the programs adopted in the dictatorship of the proletariat and the new relationships and possibilities established. These characteristics cannot exist—and one should not expect to find them—before this context itself has developed in ways that the world has yet to experience. Likewise, the extraordinary qualities Marx ascribes to the people of communism could never exist outside of the unique conditions which give rise to them, and given these conditions the development of other qualities, certainly of opposing qualities, simply makes no sense. One can only state the unproven assumptions on which this expected flowering of human nature rests: that the individual's potential is so varied and so great; that he possesses an inner drive to realize all this potential; that the whole range of powers in each person can be fully realized together; and that the overall fulfillment of each individual is compatible with that of all others. Given how often and drastically the development and discovery of new social forms has extended accepted views of what is human, I think it would be unwise at this time to foreclose on the possibility that Marx's assumptions are correct.

There is really only one way to evaluate Marx's vision of communism and that is to examine his analysis of capitalism to see if the communist society is indeed present within it as an unrecognized potentiality. If Marx sought, as he tells us, "to find the new world through the criticism of the old," then any judgement of his views on communism rests in the last analysis on the validity of his critique of capitalism. This is not the place for the extensive examination that is required, but I would like to offer three guidelines to those who would undertake it: (1) capitalism must be conceptualized in terms of social relations, Marx's way of incorporating the actual past and future possibilities of his subject into his study of its present forms (this is the logical basis of Marx's study of history, including future history, as a process); (2) a Marxist analysis of today's capitalism should be integrated into the study of Marx's analysis of late nineteenth century capitalism (the social relations from which projections are made must be brought up to date); and (3) one should not try to show that communism is inevitable, only that it is possible, that it is based on conditions inherent in the further development of our present ones. After all, communism is never opposed because one holds other values, but because it is said to be an unrealizable ideal. In these circumstances, making a case for communism as a *possible* successor to capitalism is generally enough to convince people that they must help to bring it about.[128]

Maurice Meisner is a professor of history at the University of Wisconsin at Madison. A student of Maoist theory, Professor Meisner has written extensively on the origins and development of Mao Tse-tung Thought, including Li Ta-chao and the Origins of Chinese Marxism *(Harvard University Press),* "Leninism and Maoism: Some Populist Perspectives on Marxism-Leninism in China" (China Quarterly), *and* The People's Republic of China: An Interpretative History of the Maoist Era—*a study which will be published in the spring of this year. Professor Meisner has also coedited a collection of essays entitled* The Mozartian Historian: Essays on the Works of Joseph R. Levenson.

4

Utopian and Dystopian Elements in the Maoist Vision of the Future

Maurice Meisner

Lewis Mumford once observed that the term "utopia" can be taken to mean either the ultimate in human hope or the ultimate in human folly. He also noted that Sir Thomas More—whose famous book introduced the modern word—was aware of both meanings when he pointed to the divergent Greek origins of the term: *eutopia,* which means the good place; and *outopia,* which means no place.[1]

In the case of Mao Tse-tung—and it is the case of the most celebrated utopian prophet of our age—one encounters a vision of the future which contains both *eutopia* and *outopia.* On the one hand, Mao prophesizes the advent of socialism and communism, a vision derived from the ultimate goals set forth in Marxist theory. On the other hand, Mao's communist utopia appears as only a transient phenomenon in what he envisions to be an endless process of change beyond communism which leads nowhere, or more precisely, an ahistorical cosmic process which results in the end of history, the end of man, and indeed the destruction of the universe. In the Maoist vision one finds both a future and a nonfuture, both a utopian and a dystopian projection of the contradictions of the present into an almost theological vision of "the end of days." This paper is intended as a preliminary inquiry into the history and nature of the Maoist vision of the future and an attempt to evaluate the function of both its utopian and dystopian strains in contemporary Chinese historical development.

Before turning to utopianism in contemporary China, it might be in order to offer a few prefatory comments on the treatment of utopianism in the contemporary West. For in view of the widespread hostility to utopian thought and impulses in Western scholarship, a Western observer of utopianism in a non–Western land should make some attempt to clarify his own views and biases on the general subject at the outset.

Preface

"Utopia," both "the good place" and "no place." For the most part, it would seem, Western scholars prefer the latter meaning and have ignored the former. That which is "utopian," as the term is commonly employed, is that which is in principle unrealizable—and thus it follows that those who strive to achieve the "impossible" are, at best, hopeless day dreamers in search of "no place," and more often than not, dangerous fanatics prone to the most irrational actions. It is very much in the mainstream of contemporary Western thought and scholarship to contrast (and condemn) the "utopian" mode of thinking to that which is celebrated as "rational," "realistic," "sober," and "empirical." Thus we constantly are warned to beware of the danger of the intrusion of utopian visions and messianic prophecies in the pragmatic and secular realm of politics, and we are encouraged to applaud the demise of utopian aspirations and ideologies and to deplore their survivals and revivals. The widespread influence of the profoundly antiutopian writings of J. L. Talmon, Norman Cohn, Adam Ulam, and those associated with the school of thought which proclaimed (prematurely, it would seem) "the end of ideology," testifies to the dominant Western scholarly view that utopian strivings are not

only strivings to reach "no place" but also politically dangerous and historically pernicious.

We are dealing here, of course, with much more than the
semantic problem of what the term "utopianism" means.
The meanings and implications that are given to it and the
different ways in which it is employed in describing and
interpreting sociohistorical phenomena reflect fundamentally
differing attitudes toward historical change in general, differing perceptions of how, where, and in what direction
history has, is, or should be moving—and most directly, assumptions about the role of revolution in modern history.
For if revolutions are inspired by utopian hopes, then it is
only logical that those who condemn utopianism should
also condemn revolution. Thus Cohn finds in the "revolutionary messianism" of medieval Europe the source of much
of modern revolutionary history since the seventeenth
century, the "prologue to the vast revolutionary upheavals
of the present century," and the harbinger of modern totalitarianism.[2] Talmon argues that it was the "political messianism" of eighteenth century French thought which gave
birth to both "Jacobin and Marxist conceptions of the
Utopia," releasing a "revolutionary spirit" of "totalitarian
democracy" that eventually spent itself in Western Europe
but was destined to "spread eastwards until it found its
natural home in Russia."[3] And we can move further east-
ward with Adam Ulam who has argued that in the modern
West "the utopian character of much of socialist thinking
represented . . . a kind of rearguard action which withdrawing
radicalism conducted against the triumphant march of industrialism and liberalism."[4] The revolutionary utopian menace
now comes from the vast non-Western areas of the world
where radical utopianism has "withdrawn" and where industrialism and liberalism have yet to triumph. For, as Ulam
candidly and rhetorically queries, is not "all of utopian thinking and much of socialist thought but a critique of the values
and traditions of the West?"[5]

A condemnation of utopianism linked to a general antirevolutionary bias—and particularly to the perceived threat of

the combination of the two in the non-Western world—are
themes in contemporary Western writings too familiar to
require discussion here.[6] To be sure, there is a rich and
continuing tradition of scholarly literature which treats
utopianism in a more historically and humanly sympathetic
fashion.[7] But the analytic and historical insights that might
be gained from these works—and there is a growing scholarly
interest in the general subject of utopian and messianic movements—have yet to be much applied to Chinese historical
experience in general and seem to have made virtually no
impact at all on those who write on contemporary China.
A survey of the literature on the latter, it is fair to say, would
reflect the dominant antiutopian and antirevolutionary
proclivities noted above and, correspondingly, a high value
placed on the virtues of social "stability" and "equilibrium."
In the context of the postrevolutionary Chinese situation,
these are translated into a preference for the assumed virtues
of "instrumental rationality," "bureaucratic professionalism," and processes of "institutionalization" in general.
Unfortunately, the question of what is or what might or
should be "institutionlized" is rarely raised. Thus when one
reads references to such terms as "Maoist utopianism" or
"Mao's vision," one is being told, or is likely to assume, that
some element of abnormal or irrational behavior is involved.

In attempting to employ "utopianism" as a general sociohistorical concept, it clearly is of no analytic value to use the
term, as is commonly the case, simply in a vaguely descriptive manner with generally pejorative connotations. More
fruitful for historical analysis is to understand utopianism,
as Karl Mannheim has defined it, as a mode of thought which
is "incongruous with the state of reality within which it
occurs," as an orientation which "transcends reality and
which at the same time breaks the bonds of the existing
order."[8] Without accepting Mannheim's rather misleading
distinction between "utopia" and "ideology," if for no other
reason than that one can quite legitimately speak of "utopian
ideologies," there are many insights to be gained from
Mannheim's analysis of the general sociohistorical role of

"the utopian mentality." Especially pertinent for the present discussion is an understanding of the revolutionary function of utopianism, the manner in which certain modes of thought and conceptions of the future clash with existing reality and thereby give rise to activities which tend to transcend and transform the world in accordance with an image of what it should be.[9] Here it is of particular importance to appreciate the historically dynamic role of one of the enduring features of human historical experience—the tension, to quote Weber, between "the actually existent and the ideal."[10] Such tension between what are perceived to be the imperfections and evils of the world as it is and a conception of what the world should be is a characteristic—and indeed essential—feature of utopian and messianic mentalities in general, appearing both in religious and secular ideologies. This sense of tension, however, does not necessarily lead to historically significant forms of action; it may well result (perhaps more often than not) in attempts to withdraw from the sordid world in a search for individual salvation, or become dissipated in salvationist-type religious ideologies which promise relief and "the good life" in the hereafter. What determines whether the tension generated by utopian aspirations gives rise to effective and dynamic forces of change depends upon particular sociohistorical circumstances. Briefly following Weber on this point,[11] one can identify three essential prerequisites. First, the tension that flows from a utopian conception of what the world should be must find a place in a comprehensive world view which aims at a "collective revolutionary transformation of the world in the direction of a more ethical status" and which at the same time sanctions values freed from tradition and thus orients human conduct in an innovative fashion toward the achievement of the utopian goal in this world and in the here and now. Secondly, prophetic and utopian ideologies and world views become truly dynamic and "reality-transcending" factors in historical process only when they become identified with the particular social and psychological needs of politically and economically oppressed and disprivileged social groups rather than when they serve as ideological justifications for the privileges of dominant classes and for the preservation of existing social orders. Finally, it follows from the above that what is crucial for understanding the sociohistorical significance of utopian and messianic movements is not only the character of the prophet and the content of his prophecy but also the mass response to them. Prophetic messages and utopian appeals are of little historical interest if no one is listening. It is "the nature of the values held by the mass of the followers," Peter Worsley has observed, that is of primary significance in understanding how prophets "are able to mobilize support readily, or, in some cases, even to have support thrust upon them."[12] Thus, however important and interesting the personality of the prophet, the focus of attention ultimately must be on the nature of the relationship between leader and followers. As Worsley has suggested, the valid analytic model has to be "interactionist" in nature; that is, "one in which followers with possibly utopian or at least diffuse and unrealized aspirations cleave to an appropriate leader because he articulates and consolidates their aspirations."[13] In somewhat different terms, the problem posed here is that of determining the circumstances under which (as Bendix has put it) "the inspirations of a few become the convictions of the many."[14]

An appreciation of the general historical significance of utopianism is expressed in particularly insightful fashion in Frederick Polak's summary of the role of what he calls "images of the future" in historical development:

First and most important is man's emerging time-schizophrenia, his dualistic mental capacity to imagine another and radically different world and time. An elite of spiritual leaders and visionary messengers enter on the scene. They create positive images of a future better than the present. Certain of these images, which happen to combine intellectual insights and esthetic appeal in such a way as to strike emotional resonance with the social and mental needs of the time, arouse great enthusiasm in the masses. Society is then fired by the force of these dominating visions which draw men toward that other and better future. The promises inhering in the visions burst through the historical past-present and break open the hidden present-future. In the process, some of them are seized upon and, as it were, "chosen" by society out of a great many possible futures and harnessed to the present. These images of the future have formed one of the main driving forces of cultural dynamics and have been playing a preponderant role, through their alternating strength and weakness, in the rise and fall of civilization.[15]

It is with this kind of historical perspective that one can more fruitfully understand the revolutionary historical role of utopianism and perhaps better appreciate Mannheim's well-known comment that "with the relinquishment of utopias, man would lose his will to shape history and therewith his ability to understand it"[16] and Weber's historical truism that "man would not have attained the possible unless time and again he had reached out for the impossible."[17]

Leaving aside the complex question of the relationship between the utopian prophet and his followers and the more general problem of the social origins of, and the mass response to, utopian prophets and prophecies, it is necessary at this point to clarify and roughly define "the utopian mentality," as that term will be used in the present essay and applied to Maoism. Without entering into the problem of attempting to catalogue and classify the many varieties of utopias and utopian modes of thought and movements, it is useful to distinguish religious, messianic conceptions, and movements of a generally salvationist character on the one hand from secular forms of utopianism on the other. This is not to deny that the two may share certain common characteristics, that the comparative study of the two may provide insights for the understanding of both, nor that millennial and messianic religious movements and ideas may have profound influences on historical development or may in fact take on a secular, political form. Nonetheless, there is a general (if not always completely clear) line of demarcation between messianic or millennial salvationist creeds and secular utopianism. Here we are concerned with the latter. A much more important distinction to keep in mind is that between passive or contemplative utopianism on the one hand and activistic utopianism on the other. In the former case, one is dealing with essentially literary descriptions of the good or perfect society, a long tradition of utopian thought that goes back to Plato (in the Western tradition), constantly reappears as an enduring strain through the Middle Ages, in Thomas More's famous work, in the various nature utopias of the eighteenth century, in the flood of "utopian socialist" schemes and blueprints which emerged in the early industrial era, and which in various forms (new and old) continue to the present day. To be sure, this tradition of passivistic utopianism is not without significant historical influences and implications. But certainly of far greater historical importance—and obviously more relevant for understanding the Maoist mentality—is the activistic form of utopianism which combines a vision of the good society with a demand to achieve it by concrete political and social action. As a rough working definition for the purposes of the present essay, the secular and activist utopian mentality can be characterized by

1. not only a vision of a more or less perfect society located in the future but a chiliastic expectation that its advent is more or less imminent in the process of becoming;
2. a conviction that men can create the new and perfect order by their own actions in the here and now;
3. an extraordinary sense of tension between the world as it is and as it is conceived that it ought to be;
4. flowing from above, a demand for collective political action to transform society in accordance with the utopian vision of what it ought to be;
5. a totalistic conception of the forthcoming revolutionary transformation, both in the sense that it is conceived as a complete and radical change of existing conditions and in the sense that it demands the transformation of the social world as a whole; the notion that the new social order can be brought about through the establishment of small, ideal communities (or communes) to serve

simply as models for emulation is regarded as wholly insufficient.

It also should be noted that strongly antitraditional impulses and implications are generally characteristic of utopian mentalities. The envisioned new society is generally accompanied by a demand for a radical break with the traditional norms, values, and customs associated with the old order. This emphasis on the abandonment of the past in general is commonly expressed through themes of rebirth which appear so prominently in utopian-type ideologies and through the notion that the emergence of the new society will bring forth (or presupposes) the appearance of "new men" with a wholly new morality. Asceticism is also a typical feature of utopian as well as messianic modes of thought. While the ideology may promise a future of plenty, ascetic acts and values of self-denial, struggle, and sacrifice are generally seen as the means to arrive at that future.

Before considering the Maoist version of Marxism as a form of utopianism, a few words should be said about the common assumption that there is some necessary causal relationship between utopian thought and totalitarian politics. The usual—and quite influential—argument is that any ideology which proclaims a highly utopian vision of the future is in part responsible for, and an essential feature of, modern totalitarianism in general and (in the form of a messianic commitment to Marxian utopian goals) for communist totalitarianism in particular. As Talmon has so forcefully argued, at the root of modern totalitarian tyranny is a special "messianic temperament" which postulates the inevitable coming of "a perfect scheme of things."[18] According to this view, the most repressive features of contemporary communist states can be explained, in large measure, in terms of the acceptance of the Marxist apocalyptic promise of the universal advent of a totally egalitarian society; totalitarian domination in the present is not only justified but also essentially determined by a belief in necessary laws of historical development inevitably leading to worldwide salvation. Thus communist totalitarianism is a "secularized sociopolitical religion" based on the "utopian eschatology" of Karl Marx.[19] This, of course, is one of the central assumptions of the widely accepted "totalitarian model" of communism. It may be recalled, for example, that the first of the five characteristic features which Carl Friedrich attributes to "all totalitarian societies" is "an official ideology . . . characteristically focused in terms of chiliastic claims as to the 'perfect' final society of mankind."[20]

Here we are dealing not merely with a view of utopianism as the ultimate in human folly (although that too is assumed) but utopianism seen as a darkly sinister force in modern history. We are also dealing, in part, with what Michael Walzer has so incisively noted to be "that easy and false equation of radicalism and totalitarianism which has become so common among historians, sociologists and political scientists in the last 15 or 20 years."[21] It is precisely because it is so easy— and thus so common—to assume that radical utopianism necessarily has sinister political implications that makes it so difficult to discuss the historical role of utopianism without condemning it from the beginning. It is easy because there is some obvious general historical truth in the proposition that men seized by utopian visions of a perfect future—and who are determined to bring about that future—are likely to feel morally free to employ the most immoral means to reach the desired (and presumably inevitable) end. Yet to accept this seeming truism for the purposes of historical generalization is to distort one's perspective on utopianism from the outset.

While it is well beyond the scope of this essay to offer a critique of the notion that there is some necessary causal relationship between utopianism and totalitarianism, it might be observed that it is also historically true that totalitarian polities and societies (both modern and premodern) can and have existed without utopian ideologies and impulses. There are obviously many historical conditions which tend to produce totalitarianism (ranging from external threats and wars to various kinds of internal socioeconomic crises) and it is altogether too simplistic to believe that the crucial factor always lurking in the background is a special messianic-utopian temperament. Here it might suffice to take note of two modern historical examples. In the case of China itself, it is well to keep in mind that the pronounced totalitarian character of Kuomintang rule (both before 1949 and in Taiwan since 1949) was in no sense accompanied by any utopian ideology or aspirations—or, for that matter, even by any serious program for social change. Perhaps more pertinent for the present discussion is the history of the Soviet Union. Here it might be observed that the Marxian utopian themes and promises which Lenin invoked on the eve of the Bolshevik Revolution (most notably in *State and Revolution*) and during the early months of the Soviet experience tended to disappear from his speeches and writings after mid-1918—precisely at the time that the Soviet state was becoming increasingly bureaucratic and oppressive. And it might further be noted that Stalinist Russia (the major example for the entire totalitarian model) is the classic case of the rituali-zation of utopian goals. The manner in which Stalin "post-poned" Marxist goals, turned them into empty rituals, and cynically manipulated them to rationalize the policies of a brutal bureaucratic-totalitarian regime is a matter too well known to require elaboration here. What makes the common association between utopianism and totalitarianism so questionable is precisely the failure to distinguish between genuine utopianism and the ritualization of utopia. Yet this distinction is essential for any serious sociohistorical analysis of utopianism, and especially so for understanding the nature and role of the Maoist utopian mentality.

The History of the Maoist Vision

During the revolutionary years, there was nothing at all utopian about the Maoist vision of the future. In his pre-1949 writings, Mao said little about the postrevolutionary future, and on the rare occasions he did refer to socialism and com-munism, he spoke in only the most vague and general terms. Indeed, his vision seems to have been a most prosaic one, as in 1938 when he responded to an English correspondent's query about his conception of the new China: "Every man has food to eat and clothes to wear. Every man understands the rights and duties of citizenship and has a fair chance of education and amusement. The marriage customs are to be reformed, roads built, industry developed, a six-hour day established. There is no foreign aggression. No man oppresses another. There is equality and freedom and universal love. Together all [will] build the peace of the world."[22]

The Chinese Communist victory of 1949 itself was not accompanied by the same chialistic revolutionary expectations and utopian visions which had marked the Russian Bolshevik Revolution of 1917. The anticlimactic consummation of a prolonged revolutionary process which had taken place in the rural hinterlands of China, the peculiarly insular character of the revolution and the mentality of its leaders, the long period of Chinese isolation from international revolutionary currents (and indeed the absence of any international revolutionary situation), and the continued Maoist insistence on the "bourgeois" character of the revolution itself—all were factors which militated against the emergence of any utopian expectations that military and political victory portended the imminent advent of a perfect order of justice and equality. Mao Tse-tung, to be sure, celebrated the revolutionary victory by reaffirming that the eventual communist aim was to realize the Marxist goal of a classless society, but he did so only to postpone that goal to a vaguely indefinite time in the future and to dampen such utopian hopes as the Communist victory may have aroused in Chinese society and among the cadres of the Chinese Communist Party. Ultimate Marxist goals, as Mao put it at the time, merely were "mentioned in passing" and were to be seen only in terms of "the long-range perspective of human progress." In the meantime, and for the foreseeable future, energies were to be turned to more immediate, realistic, and tangible tasks—the building of a strong state and a strong economy.[23] "Three years of recovery, ten years of development," was the slogan with which the history of the People's

Republic began, and it reflected the relatively sober temper of the time.

It was entirely in harmony with the celebrated "pragmatic" character of Maoist revolutionary strategy that Mao and the Chinese Communist leaders formulated their strategy for postrevolutionary development. Unlike Lenin in 1917, Mao in 1949 was not burdened by any utopian expectations of a global socialist revolutionary process and thus the postponement of specifically socialist goals was easily accomplished— and, indeed, taken for granted from the beginning. Nor did Mao harbor any of Lenin's anguished doubts about the historical viability and moral validity of attempting to build a socialist society in conditions of economic and social backwardness. For Mao and the Chinese Communists, the overcoming of backwardness was viewed as an enormous practical task to be undertaken; it did not present them with any Marxist theoretical dilemmas to be resolved—partly, perhaps, because unlike their Russian counterparts they never were intellectually committed to genuine Marxist perspectives on the economic, social, and cultural prerequisites for socialism. Moreover, the Soviet historical experience, it was believed at the time, provided the appropriate model to be adopted and emulated—the historical model which demonstrated how to industrialize an economically backward country under socialist political auspices and the model for a noncapitalist path to socialism. However much the Chinese Communists had come to distrust and defy Stalin's "guidance" during the revolutionary years, they apparently had no reservations about the validity of the Stalinist strategy of postrevolutionary development. And although Mao long had warned against "the mechanical absorption of foreign material" (as he put it in 1940), he proved remarkably uncritical during the early 1950s in accepting and adopting the Stalinist strategy of economic development. Nor is there any evidence that he had any doubts at the time about Stalinist means of economic development leading to the desired socialist ends. The question whether the Soviet Union was a socialist society or not was not debated: it was simply assumed. Although the

Chinese Communists knew little about the nature of Soviet society other than what they had read in official Stalinist textbooks, it was then a prime article of the Maoist faith that Russia was "the land of socialism," and, as Mao proclaimed in 1949, "a great and glorious socialist state." "Learn from the Soviet Union" was the guiding Maoist slogan during the early years of the People's Republic as the Communists strove to revive an economy ravaged by decades of foreign invasion and civil war and to establish political order and national unity after a century of disintegration. And, at the end of 1952, the slogan was translated into China's First Five Year Plan (1953–57), a plan based on the wholesale adoption of Stalinist methods, techniques, and ideological assumptions.

Even without the benefit of historical hindsight, it seems strange that the Chinese Communists should have embraced so ardently and uncritically the ready-made Soviet model. Having come to power through a revolutionary strategy that abandoned many Stalinist orthodoxies—and indeed in direct defiance of Stalin's political authority—they now quickly and uncritically accepted Stalin's authority as an economic strategist and as the "builder of socialism." Having emerged from a rural revolutionary environment where they had worked out their own distinctive patterns of thought and organization, they now turned their backs on their unique revolutionary heritage in favor of a program of rapid urban industrialization which demanded the subordination of agriculture to modern industry and the exploitation of the countryside for the benefit of the cities. And it was Mao, the most unorthodox of the Chinese Communists during the revolutionary years, who took the lead in promoting the orthodox Stalinist strategy of development during the early postrevolutionary years.

Since Chinese industrialization proceeded largely in accordance with Soviet-borrowed methods and techniques, it is hardly surprising that the process gave rise to similar social and ideological tendencies. The social results of China's First Five Year Plan are well known: the emergence of new administrative and technological elites; growing inequalities among the urban working class and the subjection of workers to an increasingly harsh and repressive labor discipline; a stronger and more oppressive state apparatus presided over by an increasingly bureaucratized Communist Party; and a widening economic and cultural gap between the modernizing cities and the backward countryside.

And, as in the Soviet case, the growth of new patterns of social inequality was accompanied by a familiar process of the postponement and ritualization of Marxian social goals. To be sure, when the Communists formally launched the First Five Year Plan at the beginning of 1953 they also announced the inauguration of the era of "the transition to socialism." But while the pursuit of modern industrial development was clear enough, the meaning of socialism became increasingly ambiguous.   Chinese society seemed to be moving further away from, rather than closer to, the socialist future that the revolution had promised to bring. Modern industrial development was conceived as the means to achieve socialist ends, but the logic of the process soon made industrialization itself the primary goal while socialist visions were postponed to an ever more distant future and tended to become ritualized into slogans to spur production. This eminently Stalinist pattern was also eminently Maoist at the time, for Mao then fully accepted the Marxist-Leninist orthodoxy that a high level of the development of the material forces of production was the essential precondition for the socialist transformation of society. Socialism and communism required a long and indefinite period of preparation, it was emphasized, and no one emphasized the point more strongly than Mao.   He hardly could have been described as a utopian visionary at the time. Neither the theory nor the practice of the Chinese Communists in the early years of the People's Republic foreshadowed the utopian and apocalyptic impulses which eventually were to throw the postrevolutionary order into new revolutionary convulsions.

What is unique and extraordinary about the postrevolutionary history of China is the emergence of a powerful revolutionary utopianism long after the new order had become consolidated, routinized, and seemingly institutionalized. The contrast with Soviet history is, of course, striking. In Russia, the Bolsheviks had come to power with highly utopian expectations—hopes and expectations which soon faded and died as Soviet society underwent a familiar and presumably inevitable process of what Robert Tucker has termed "deradicalization." In China, by contrast, the Communists came to power as rather sobered realists, determined to achieve the mundane goals of political unity and modern economic development. And they found on hand—and quickly took into their hands—the ready-made Soviet model of development that was so eminently suited to the pursuit of these eminently nationalist goals. And it was entirely in keeping with the Chinese perspectives of the time that the adopted foreign model came with built-in ideological rationalizations for the postponement of Marxist social goals. It was not until almost a decade after the revolutionary victory that what we now know as the Maoist vision appeared on the historical scene to divert China from the Soviet path and to create a unique (and turbulent) Chinese pattern of postrevolutionary history. More precisely, it was only with the Great Leap Forward campaign of 1958–60 that observers of contemporary China discovered the Maoist vision and it was during that profoundly utopian episode that the vision received its fullest and most pristine expression.

The prehistory of the Great Leap—and the period crucial for the emergence of Mao as a utopian visionary—began with Mao's July 1955 speech on agricultural collectivization and concluded (after the conclusion of the Hundred Flowers era) in late 1957 with the triumph of distinctively Maoist socioeconomic policies. Without entering into the complex political struggles and policy conflicts which marked these years, it might be noted that the emerging Maoist vision involved a wholesale rejection of the Soviet developmental model and is closely bound up with the whole phenomenon of the cult of Mao, with its profoundly antibureaucratic and anti-Leninist implications.

Mao's July 1955 speech was more than an attempt to overcome socioeconomic stagnation in the countryside. It marked not only the beginning of the Maoist abandonment of Stalinist assumptions (at least in the realm of socioeconomic change), but also the postponement of socialist goals as immediate goals to be actively striven for in the here and now, coupled with a new-found faith in the peasantry as the main agency of the forthcoming socialist transformation. It also was the first in a series of personal policy initiatives on the part of Mao which were to set him above the Communist Party as a supreme leader—and utopian prophet—who could speak directly to "the people" (and especially the peasants) and speak for them as well. Mao single-handedly dissolved the Party consensus on agrarian policy and launched the intensive drive for agricultural collectivization in a manner unprecedented in the history of the Chinese Communist Party—and in a manner that set a precedent to be followed in more radical fashion in the Great Leap Forward campaign and the Cultural Revolution. The speech on "The Question of Agricultural Cooperation" was delivered not to the Party central committee, where Mao was in a minority at the time, but rather to an informal gathering of provincial and regional Party secretaries who happened to be in Peking for a session of the National People's Congress. In effect, Mao overrode and overruled his own central committee and appealed to rural Party cadres at large, and through them to the rural masses, to follow his new and distinctively rural path to socialism.

A matter of utmost significance for understanding the emergence of the Maoist vision as an active force in social development—and the emergence of Mao as a utopian prophet leading China to the realization of that vision—was the way in which Mao perceived the relationship between the peasant masses and the Leninist party, a perception which harkened back to the famous "Hunan Report" of 1927 and one which served to revive much of the populist spirit and imagery of the latter. In 1927 he had found the true sources of revolutionary creativity to reside not in the Party but rather in the spontaneous movement of the peasantry acting on its own. It was not the Party that was to judge the revolutionary capacities of the peasants—although Mao himself might possess the capacity to make such judgements—but rather it was the action of the peasants themselves which was to serve as the criterion for judging the revolutionary capacity of the Party.[24] Again in 1955 Mao counterposed a revolutionary peasantry to a party that was insufficiently revolutionary. While Mao described most peasants as striving to achieve radical social change (and, indeed, soon were to be seen as filled with an inherent desire for socialism), he complained that Party members were "tottering along like a woman with bound feet." "As things stand today," he declared, "the mass movement is in advance of the leadership"—and party officials who argued that collectivization was proceeding too rapidly and had gone beyond the understanding of the masses merely revealed their own lack of faith in the masses.[25]

Here we find the implicit claim that only Mao himself, not the Party as such, best represents the desires and interests of the peasant masses. It is this claim which set the stage for the emergence of the Maoist vision as an active force in policy-making and the emergence of Mao as the sole prophet of a new agrarian road to socialism.

The new Maoist formulae for economic development and socialist transformation were set forth in his 1956 (nonpublic) speech "On the Ten Great Relationships," which explicitly repudiated the Soviet model and China's First Five Year Plan.[26] But Mao's proposals were opposed by most Party leaders and, as he later complained, largely ignored. They were to be accepted and implemented only in late 1957, after Mao had turned the Hundred Flowers campaign and its "antirightist" aftermath into a movement to break down the resistance of state and party bureaucrats to the radical socioeconomic policies he was advocating. The abortiveness of the Hundred Flowers campaign and its results are crucial for understanding how the Maoist vision came into historical play. Without going into the controversial question of the motives behind the campaign, much less the history of the movement itself, one might take note of two essential (and novel) propositions advanced in Mao's major theoretical treatise of the period, his February 1957 speech "On the Correct Handling of Contradictions Among the People." (The speech, of course, served a dual function; it served to revive the Hundred Flowers movement—and then, when it was published in revised form in June 1957, also served to justify the suppression of the critics who had been invited to "bloom and contend.") First, we find here the proposition that contradictions between leaders and led still remain in a presumably socialist society, the corollary view that the Chinese Communist Party is not infallible, and the conclusion that it is therefore permissible and desirable for "the people" to criticize the Party from without. The implications of this argument for the position of Mao—and for the activation of his "vision"—were profoundly important, for if the people in general were now free to criticize the Party, then who was to speak for "the people" in general if not Mao himself; Mao, after all, was not only the chairman of the Party, but also the head of the people's government—and, more importantly, as acknowledged leader of the people's revolution, he possessed special bonds to the masses no one else could claim. Thus if the people were now free to speak, then Mao was their preeminent spokesman. What the argument did, in brief, was to free Mao from the Leninist discipline of the Party and enable him to criticize it from without in his uniquely transcendent role as the representative of the will of the people.

Secondly, the supremacy of Mao was reinforced by the proposition that class struggles continue under socialism and take a primarily ideological form, termed as a "class struggle in the ideological field between the proletariat and the bourgeoisie." The doctrine had ominous implications for Mao's political opponents within the Party, for if "class struggle" was now a matter of struggle between class ideologies rather than between actual social classes, if the Party and its leaders were no longer ideologically infallible and indeed susceptible to bourgeois ideological influences, then ideological and policy conflicts within the Party were to be seen as social class conflicts. The Party itself thus becomes the political arena where the "class struggle" between the "proletariat" and the "bourgeoisie" is fought out, with Mao obviously the principal spokesman for the former.

While the profoundly non-Leninist implications of these notions only became fully explicit in the Cultural Revolution, they also played a critical role in the late 1957 Party debates on socioeconomic policy, debates where Mao, partly standing above the Party, proved victorious. It was this victory which led to the implementation of the Maoist vision early the following year in the form of the Great Leap Forward campaign.

In the Great Leap era, Mao appeared on the historical scene as a utopian prophet appealing and speaking directly to the masses, and especially the peasant masses, partly bypassing regular Party and bureaucratic channels in what became a gigantic mass movement with strong utopian and chiliastic overtones, promising as it did the rapid transition from socialism to communism. It was a great *tour de force* on the part of Mao in which he established for a time a direct spiritual bond between himself and the people, a bond between his own utopian visions and popular aspirations for radical social and economic change. The movement, of course, was accompanied by an enormous glorification of both the person and the "thought" of Mao Tse-tung.

It was during the period of the Great Leap Forward that the Maoist vision of the future received its fullest and most pristine expression in theory. And it also was the time which saw the most ambitious attempt to realize that vision in social practice. On the whole, it was a period marked by a positive utopianism and a highly optimistic vision of the future. Three years of struggle would be followed by a thousand years of happiness, it was promised, and it was envisioned that China would overtake and surpass the economic levels of the most advanced industrialized countries within fifteen years. But it was not simply a good material life that Maoists promised, for they conceived the Great Leap as more than a crash program for modernization. It was also proclaimed to be the period of the transition from socialism to communism. The ultimate goals of classical Marxism, hitherto postponed to an indefinite time in the future, now became immediate goals to be undertaken in the here and now. The rural communes were to bring about not only productivity miracles but a social miracle as well—the leap to a communist utopia based on the principle of "to each according to his needs." They were to begin the work of abolishing the distinctions between town and countryside, between mental and manual labor, and between workers, peasants, and intellectuals—and indeed even the abolition of the internal functions of the state. And the work to realize these utopian socially revolutionary tasks was to begin at once; they were conceived and popularized not as distant ends dependent on the prior development of the necessary material forces of production but rather as immediate tasks of the day to be pursued and implemented (at least in embryonic form) in the very process of constructing the Marxian-defined material preconditions for their realization. Through combining industry and agriculture in what was perceived as an ideologically and spiritually pure rural setting—and with a deep faith in the inherent socialist aspirations of the masses and in the powers of human consciousness to mold reality in accordance with its dictates—it was envisioned that the building of a communist society and the development of a modern economy could proceed simultaneously. The conditions of communism and its preconditions, it was assumed, would prove mutually reinforcing, and thus the ends and means of communism would be reconciled.

The Great Leap Forward vision of the future was derived from classical Marxist sources. The communes, it was typically proclaimed at the time, were paving the way

> to the gradual transition from the socialist principle of "to each according to his work" to the Communist principle of "to each according to his needs," the way to the gradual dimunition and

final elimination of the differences between rural and urban areas, between worker and peasant and between mental and manual labor, and the way to the gradual dimunition and final elimination of the domestic functions of the state. . . . It can also be foreseen that in the future Communist society, the people's commune will remain the basic unit of the social structure.[27]

In depicting their vision of the future, Maoists drew heavily on the more utopian strains in the Marxist tradition. Nothing was more frequently quoted in the theoretical and popular literature of the Great Leap era than the famous passage in *The German Ideology* where Marx took one of his rare glimpses into the future and saw a communist society "where nobody has one exclusive sphere of activity, but each can become accomplished in any branch he wishes," a society which "regulates the general production and thus makes it possible for me to do one thing today and another tomorrow, to hunt in the morning, fish in the afternoon, rear cattle in the evening, criticize after dinner, just as I have a mind, without ever becoming hunter, fisherman, shepherd or critic." This idyllic and almost pastoral vision of communism was entirely in harmony with the Maoist expectation of the time that "new men" of "all-round" abilities would soon produce a society where "everyone will be a mental laborer and at the same time a physical laborer. Everyone can be a philosopher, scientist, writer, or artist." Also widely propagated in the Great Leap literature were passages from Marx's *Civil War in France* and Lenin's *State and Revolution,* for the model of the Paris Commune was seen as relevant to the contemplated decentralization of state power to the rural communes which would integrate political and economic organization. The communes were envisioned as instruments of "the dictatorship of the proletariat," the agencies which would carry out the transition from socialism to communism and achieve a classless and stateless society.[28]

While the social goals proclaimed in the Great Leap vision were Marxist-inspired, the means to achieve them were not. There is, of course, nothing either Marxist or Leninist in the Maoist belief that the truly creative forces for revolutionary social change reside in the countryside rather than the cities, in the faith that the power of the human spirit is the decisive factor in bringing about the new society, or in the assumption that "the transition from socialism to communism" can be accomplished in conditions of economic scarcity. The latter notion received its most extreme formulation in the Maoist celebration of the revolutionary virtues of being "poor and blank."[29] The Great Leap Forward campaign was a profoundly utopian historical episode, utopian in the chiliastic fervors and expectations which characterized the early stages of the movement—and perhaps even more "utopian" in the pejorative Marxist sense of that term.

While the popular and public ideology of the Great Leap Forward promised the more or less imminent advent of a harmonious communist utopia, one cannot fail to note the appearance of a contradictory—and partially dystopian—strain in Mao's "private" vision. In setting forth his peculiar version of "the theory of permanent revolution" in early 1958—a theory which served as the main ideological underpinning for the Maoist economic policies of the Great Leap—Mao expounded as a universal and eternal law of historical development the notion that "disequilibrium is normal and absolute" whereas "equilibrium is temporary and relative."[30] Not only would the whole period of the "transition from socialism to communism" be characterized by a continuous series of social contradictions and class struggles, but communist society itself would be marked by a continuing process of ideological and political struggle.[31] Mao, in effect, proclaimed the permanence of conflict and denied the possibility of any definitive resolution.

The dystopian aspects of the Maoist law of "disequilibrium"—and its implications for the Maoist vision of the future—will be discussed shortly. Here it is sufficient to note that while the newly proclaimed doctrine of permanent revolution served to intensify the long-standing Maoist emphasis on the necessity and value of struggle—struggle in the social realm as

well as the struggle to conquer nature—the vision of the
future projected in the ideology of the Great Leap Forward
era was not one of endless struggle. Struggle, to be sure, was
ethically valued, but it was not an end in itself. Rather,
struggle and sacrifice in the present was justified and sanctified because it was seen as the means to realize ultimate
Marxist goals historically located in the future; the ultimate
ethical sanction for struggle and sacrifice was the promise of
a historical transformation leading to a future communist
utopia. The popular slogan "three years of struggle, a thousand years of happiness" reflected the optimistic utopian
temper of the times.

In the early phase of the Great Leap Forward movement
Mao had established himself as a utopian prophet stimulating
and articulating popular utopian expectations, a bond between his utopian visions and the peasant masses who responded to that vision. It was a posture that he was able to
maintain as long as the movement went well and promised
success, but the posture was undermined and the bond was
broken when the Great Leap ran into economic difficulties
and organizational chaos. The forced retreat from the radical
Great Leap policies resulted in the reassertion of the power
of state and Party bureaucracies and Mao's loss of real political power—and it was accompanied by widespread popular
disillusionment and, on the part of Mao, a growing pessimism
about the future. By the summer of 1959, in what was in
effect a "self-criticism," Mao no longer spoke about the
imminence of the transition to communism but rather now
began to view China's modern economic transformation as a
prolonged, century-long process: "About the people's communes, I said that they were a system of collective ownership. I said that for the transition to be completed from
collective ownership to communist ownership by the whole
people, two five-year plans was too short a period. Maybe it
will take twenty five-year plans!" "The chaos caused was on
a grand scale," he admitted, "and I take responsibility,"[32] He
even brooded over the possibility that the work of the revolution might be totally destroyed and that he might have to

begin the revolution anew. Complaining that the media had been too free in reporting errors and failures, he commented that

> if we do ten things and nine are bad, and they are all published in the press, then we will certainly perish, and we will deserve to perish. In that case, I will go to the countryside to lead the peasants to overthrow the government. If those of you in the Liberation Army won't follow me, then I will go and find a Red Army, and organize another Liberation Army.[33]

The pessimism about the future which came with the disintegration of the Great Leap Campaign deepened during the early 1960s, the "Thermidorian" years which saw the reestablishment of regular bureaucratic power and the pursuit of "revisionist" socioeconomic policies, Mao's withdrawal from day-to-day Party affairs, and a sharpening conflict between Maoists and Party bureaucrats. No longer was there any expectation of an imminent transition from socialism to communism. The vision of a "leap" from "the realm of necessity to the realm of freedom" was no longer conceived as a leap but described by Mao as a gradual process of indeterminate length.[34] The Great Leap Forward promise of an economic miracle was similarly postponed. Whereas in 1958 Mao announced that it would take only fifteen years for China to surpass the industrialized world, in 1962 he somberly concluded that "it will be impossible to develop our productive power so rapidly as to catch up with, and overtake, the most advanced capitalist countries in less than a hundred years."[35] He observed that capitalism had developed over a period of three centuries and implied that the growth of socialism and communism would take place over an equally lengthy historical era.[36]

Not only did visions of communism fade, but so did confidence in the continued viability of the existing social system. Maoists became increasingly concerned with the possibility of historical regression. "In a socialist society, new bourgeois elements may still be produced," Mao declared in January of 1962. "During the whole socialist stage there still exist classes and class struggle, and this class struggle is a protracted, complex, sometimes even violent affair."[37] And it was by no means assured that this protracted class struggle would have a favorable outcome. In the autumn of 1962 Mao raised the possibility of "the restoration of reactionary classes" and warned that "a country like ours can still move toward its opposite."[38] In the years preceding the Cultural Revolution the sense of historical indeterminateness that generally characterizes the Maoist mentality assumed darkly pessimistic overtones and implications.

It was, of course, precisely the fear that the country was turning into its "opposite," the fear that China was undergoing a "bourgeois restoration," that motivated the extraordinary events officially baptized as The Great Proletarian Cultural Revolution. In the course of that cataclysmic upheaval, Mao (as during the Great Leap era, but in more dramatic and extreme fashion) appeared on the political scene as the supreme utopian prophet issuing from above "directives" and "instructions" and "communications" to which his masses of loyal followers below were to respond and translate into revolutionary action. But if Mao again assumed the posture of utopian prophet, he was prophesizing a far different vision of the future than he had during the time of the Great Leap. The Maoist message now no longer promised an imminent era of economic abundance, much less an imminent leap to a communist utopia, but rather emphasized the need to destroy the very institutions which had been built to achieve communism, and especially the Chinese Communist Party itself. To be sure, ultimate Marxist goals were not entirely forgotten; the Cultural Revolution was depicted as part of a "proletarian" revolutionary process that eventually would abolish all forms of exploitation. But the utopian and chiliastic fervors which marked the upheaval were directed not to achieving great social ends but rather to a never-ending process of political and ideological conflict against the ever-threatening forces of "capitalist restoration" and "counterrevolution." "Destruction before construction" was the order of the day—and indeed the order of the future, for (as Mao soon proclaimed) China would require a "cultural revolution" every generation to stave off the deathly forces of revisionism and capitalism. Nor was it clear that the work of socialist construction, which presumably would follow the necessary acts of destruction, would necessarily result in any definitive Marxist resolution. For example, Liu Shao-ch'i, the principal villain and victim of the drama, was condemned (among other things) for envisioning the future communist society as one characterized by harmony and the absence of social conflict. The Cultural Revolution was dominated more by a fear of the resurrection of the forces of the past than by a positive vision of the future. And the revolutionary message Maoism now conveyed was a future of indefinite (and perhaps endless) political and ideological struggle.

The Nature and Components of the
Maoist Vision of the Future

The Maoist vision of the future is not a fixed and integrated "goal structure" which Maoists have pursued with unbending consistency over the years. The vision is composed of diverse and contradictory elements which have been combined and recombined in different ways in response to changing historical circumstances in a series of efforts to change and transcend those circumstances. In its dynamic historical interplay with differing "objective" realities, the vision has assumed different forms and the elements within it have received profoundly differing emphases. Depending on which point in historical time one chooses to select, both Maoism and the vision of the future it projects can be characterized in significantly different ways. Yet Maoism is by no means simply a series of responses to (much less reflections of) objective historical events and situations; it has been (and still remains) a powerful ideological force which has motivated men to transform the situations in which they find themselves (and to transform themselves as well) and to make history—and it has done so by conveying a utopian vision of the future and offering concrete programs of action (and a philosophy of life) to realize that future. The ends and means of Maoism form a coherent philosophic whole, albeit not necessarily an entirely consistent or unchanging one. At the risk of doing some violence to the historical dynamics and vicissitudes of the doctrine, an attempt will be made in the following pages to outline in rough and general fashion what appear to be some of the main elements of the "Maoist vision" and certain of its philosophic assumptions and theoretical implications.

A central part of the Maoist vision is certainly a Marxist-inspired conception of a future communist utopia. Maoists consistently have proclaimed their determination to achieve the classic Marxist goals of abolishing distinctions between mental and manual labor, between town and countryside, and between workers and peasants—and even the eventual "withering away" of the state. And more importantly, such goals (or at least, the first three) have been pursued with tenacity in Maoist socioeconomic policies and programs—and not without significant sociohistorical consequences. Such distinctively Maoist policies as combining industrial with agricultural production; the emphasis on the development of the agrarian sector and "the industrialization of the countryside"; educational policies and various "work-study" schemes which stress the combination of education with productive labor; the insistence that "brain workers" participate regularly in manual labor; and the vehement campaigns against bureaucracy have not created a classless society, to be sure, nor even necessarily a socialist one. But they have promoted and maintained a remarkably high degree of social egalitarianism, served to narrow the economic and cultural gap between modern cities and a backward countryside (in striking contrast to the situation characteristic of most "developing" countries), and forestalled the entrenchment of privileged strata and the stratification of bureaucratic elites. It would be impossible to explain the course of postrevolutionary socioeconomic development in the People's Republic without taking into account the Marxist components of the Maoist vision and the role they have played in determining social and political action.

Yet if Maoists are committed to the achievement of the utopian goals prophesized by Marx, they depart profoundly from the premises of both Marxism and Leninism in the means by which they conceive those goals can and should be realized. In place of the Marxian-defined economic and social prerequisites for socialism and communism, the Maoist faith in the future rests upon a reliance on the spiritual and moral transformation of men and their conscious determination and will to pursue socialist and communist ends. "If you are not completely reborn," as Mao proclaims, "you cannot enter the door of communism."[39] While both a communist consciousness and modern material conditions are to develop simultaneously in "uninterrupted" fashion, it is the "transformation of the subjective world" that is regarded as the decisive factor in "transforming the objective world." Not only do Maoists relegate objective economic conditions to a secondary status, they celebrate the moral and ideological purity they perceive to be inherent in prevailing conditions of economic backwardness—a notion which receives its most extreme formulation in Mao's thesis on the socially revolutionary virtues of being "poor and blank."

Moreover, the necessary and decisive processes of spiritual rebirth and social transformation must necessarily take place in the countryside and not in the cities. Whereas for Marx and Lenin modern history presupposed the complete dominance of town over countryside (a dominance which they considered an essential prerequisite for socialism), for Mao it is the rural areas which provide the points of departure for radical socioeconomic change. Just as Maoist revolutionary strategy rested on a faith in the revolutionary potential of the peasantry, so Maoism in the postrevolutionary era is characterized by a perception that the true sources for socialist construction reside in the rural areas. And the powerful antiurban biases which were bred during the revolutionary years remained to dominate the Maoist mentality in the postrevolutionary years. When the Communists captured the cities of China in 1949, Mao warned against the moral and ideological impurities that urban life would be likely to foster.[40] Twenty years later, he complained that the occupation of the cities was "a bad thing because it caused our Party to deteriorate."[41] The Maoist conception of an agrarian road to socialism—the belief that the potentialities for a socialist and communist future reside primarily in the peasantry and in what is perceived to be the relatively uncorrupt character of rural life—is of course a wholesale inversion of the Marxist-Leninist view of the relationship between town and countryside in the making of modern revolutionary history.

Closely associated with the emphasis on spiritual transformation and the faith in the peasantry as the necessary and appropriate means to achieve socialist ends is a general Maoist belief in the revolutionary advantages of backwardness. In his pre-Marxian world view, Mao found in China's backwardness a vast reservoir of revolutionary energy and youthful creativity that augured well for China's future,[42] and that belief remained to condition Mao's Marxist mentality through the revolutionary and postrevolutionary years and was most forcefully expressed in the "poor and blank" thesis of 1958. While economic backwardness is eventually to be eliminated, it nevertheless is perceived as the source of moral and revolutionary purity, in contrast to the economically advanced countries or the advanced areas of China where the revolutionary spirit tends to be stifled under the weight of moral decadence and political complacency. From this belief flows Mao's extraordinary revision of Marx and Lenin, boldly advanced in 1960, to the effect that "the more backward the economy, the easier [is] the transition" to socialism.[43] It is a strain in the Maoist mentality that expresses itself in the worship of youth as the bearer of a socialist future and a distrust of intellectuals as barriers to a socialist future. Just as the peasantry is seen as relatively ideologically pure because of the very virtues of its backwardness (in contrast to the inhabitants of the "advanced" cities), so youth are seen as potentially more revolutionary than their elders, because of the virtues of their very youthfulness and thus their greater amenability to moral and ideological transformation. "From ancient times the people who have created new schools of thought have always been young people without great learning," Mao declares, for "when young people grasp a truth they are invincible and old people cannot compete with them." For Mao it is a historical truism that young people "had the ability to recognize new things at a glance and having grasped them, they opened fire on the old fogeys. The old fogeys with learning always opposed them."[44]

This celebration of the creativity of youth is of course accompanied by a general Maoist distrust of intellectuals, of professionalism and expertise, and of formal education. "When the intellectuals had power, things were in a bad state [and] the country was in disorder," Mao observes, and thus "it is evident that to read too many books is harmful," for "Liu Hsiu [the founder of the Later Han dynasty who suppressed a peasant rebellion in 27 A.D.] was an academician; whereas Liu Pang [the famed peasant rebel who founded the Han dynasty in 206 B.C.] was a country bumpkin."[45] Nor is Mao's evidence drawn only from Chinese history; to support his belief that "it is not absolutely necessary to attend school," Mao notes that such creative spirits as Benjamin Franklin and Maxim Gorky had little formal education.[46] And there are of course Maoist remedies to prevent the pernicious influences of intellectuals and intellectualism: "We must drive actors, poets, dramatists and writers out of the cities, and pack them off to the countryside."[47] Moreover, "We shouldn't read too many books. We should read Marxist books, but not too many of them either. . . . If you read too many books, they petrify your mind in the end."[48] And Mao, if no longer young nor unread, nevertheless prides himself as being "a rough fellow, not cultured at all."[49]

In no area is the contrast between Maoism and Marxism more pronounced. Marx and indeed Lenin found the promise of a socialist future in the activity of the most advanced and modern social classes; they believed that socialism could be built only on the cultural as well as the material foundations of modern capitalism, and they took it for granted that the new society would inherit and appropriate all the historical accomplishments of the civilizations of the past. Mao and Maoists, by contrast, place their faith in the future in the potentialities of backwardness and the backward, look to the revolutionary spontaneity and the practical experience of the "uneducated" and the "uncultured," celebrate the virtues of being "poor and blank," and see peasants and youth as the bearers of socialism and communism.

Moreover, the Maoist road to socialism involves an enormous emphasis on the internalization of the ascetic values of struggle, self-sacrifice, and self-denial. It involves a generalization and idealization of the whole galaxy of ascetic values embodied in the model guerrilla leader of the revolutionary years. Whereas Marx regarded asceticism as the ultimate ideological expression of human self-alienation, in Maoism ascetic values receive an absolute ethical sanctification, a phenomenon closely related to the Maoist assumption that communism presupposes the presence of "new communist men." In the extreme voluntarism that characterizes the Maoist worldview, it is men imbued with the proper revolutionary spirit and moral values who are crucial to the making of history and the achievement of a communist future.

The Maoist departures from Marxism lie not simply in the "utopian" character of the means by which Maoists propose to realize communist ends, but also—and more profoundly—in the absolute normative value placed on those means and their conversion into ultimate ends. The means of Maoism are themselves integral components of the Maoist vision of the good society of the future. The moral transformation of men is not only the prerequisite for communism but part of a vision of a future that is as much a spiritual utopia as it is a social and material one. A collectivistic society based on common spiritual bonds and maintained through a ceaseless process of "ideological struggle" against the ever-present danger of the intrusion of incorrect (e.g., individualistic) thoughts is a central element in the Maoist vision of the future. The Maoist conception of the leap from "the realm of necessity" to "the realm of freedom" suggests not the Marxist image of a society conducive to the free realization of the individual human personality but rather a society whose members are in a constant struggle to internalize and practice prescribed collectivistic moral values and norms of social behavior.

Similarly, the belief that the truly creative sources of the good society of the future reside primarily in the countryside rather than in the cities involves more than making a virtue out of necessity in a predominantly agrarian country. What are perceived as the present-day virtues of peasants and rural traditions are ethically valued in themselves and projected into the Maoist conception of the future. The Maoist celebration of the rural traditions of "plain living and hard work" are seen not only as serving a utilitarian function in the present but also as components of an essentially rural utopian vision, a vision of a new society that inherits the virtues of rural life and popular peasant cultural traditions.[50]

Moreover, the antitechnocratic bias in Maoism (the distrust of intellectuals in general and technological and bureaucratic expertise in particular) reflects not only the Maoist confrontation with the dilemma of the means and ends of socialism—the fear that the growth of bureaucraticism and the emergence of a technological intelligentsia will preclude the realization of egalitarian social goals. The bias also is intimately connected with a positive image of "the new communist man," the layman "red and expert" who is a politically conscious "jack of all trades," who combines "brain work with brawn work" and masters modern technology in the course of everyday work. The ideal "red and expert" of the present, modeled on the Yenan guerrilla leader of the past, is the Maoist prototype for the "all-round" communist man of the future.

Finally, the enormous Maoist emphasis on the value and virtues of struggle and hard work are seen not simply as the means to construct the socioeconomic foundations for a communist utopia, but receive an absolute ethical sanction for all time. Struggle in behalf of the people is typically described as "saintly and divine" and the true source of all human joy and happiness. In the Maoist worldview, struggles and contradictions are both infinite and good and thus an integral part of the vision of the future.

In this conversion of the means to achieve communism into ultimate communist ends, one detects a partially dystopian strain in the Maoist mentality whereby the dominant values and tendencies of the present are projected into the vision of the future. Current conditions of economic backwardness are projected into a vision of a spiritual and rural-based utopia; cultural backwardness gives rise to a celebration of the absolute virtues of youth and the eternal creativity of the uneducated masses; and the values of the struggle and self-sacrifice to overcome backwardness themselves become absolute values and final ends. The imperatives of the present historical situation become, in effect, the goals to be realized more fully in the future.

The dystopian strain is especially pronounced in the Maoist belief in "the universality of contradiction." For Mao (and presumably for Maoists) contradictions, conflicts, and struggles are not simply the motive force of historical change but are universal and perpetual laws of nature and history. Contradiction and struggle are not only inherent in all of mankind's prehistory, but will persist under socialism and communism as well; they characterize not only the current historical epoch but exist into eternity. Mao is opposed in principle (both political and philosophic) to any notion of a harmonious and united future society.

While an enormous emphasis on contradiction and struggle has been a characteristic feature of the Maoist mentality from the beginning, it was not until relatively recently that Mao set forth the view that contradictions are permanent and ceaseless in human history. In his philosophic writings of the Yenan era, Mao equated "the law of the contradiction in things" with "the law of the unity of opposites" and envisioned that contradictions would become "nonantagonistic" in a socialist society and disappear entirely with the realization of a communist society.[51] By the late 1950s he not only was insisting on the necessity and inevitability of the continuation of class struggle under socialism but also the permanence of contradiction and conflict in the future communist society as well. In 1956 there appeared the first hint that the future would be one of ceaseless conflict: "For 10,000 years to come there will always be two sides. Each age has its two sides."[52] In 1957 Mao declared that class struggle in the "ideological field" will "never end."[53] In the following year he wrote that even after a classless society had been achieved, "ideological and political struggles between men and revolutions will continue to occur; they will never cease."[54] The law of "the unity of contradictions" no longer promised the overcoming of all contradictions in the communist future but rather dictated a future of unending struggle:

> In the communist era there will be many, many phases of development. The development from one phase to another must necessarily be a relationship between quantitative to qualitative changes. All mutations, all leaps forward are revolutions which must pass through struggles. The theory of cessation of struggles is sheer metaphysics.[55]

He later put the matter more explicitly: "When we reach Communism will there be no struggles? I don't believe that either. When we reach Communism there will still be struggles, but they will be between the new and the old, the correct and the incorrect, that is all. After tens of millennia have passed by, the incorrect will still be no good and will fail."[56]

The Maoist notion of a future of inevitable and ceaseless contradictions and struggles does not deny a progressive historical development. Socialist and communist goals will be achieved, according to Mao, in a historical process that proceeds in what he describes as a "wave-like advance" but "not as a continuously rising line,"[57] a conception that allows for periods of historical regression as well as for Mao's oft-stated belief that China can as easily revert to capitalism as move forward to socialism and communism. In the Maoist worldview, the world of history as well as the world of nature is characterized by a perpetual dialectical interaction between "equilibrium" and "disequilibrium." As Mao puts it: "The cycle, which is endless, evolves from disequilibrium to equilibrium and then to disequilibrium again. Each cycle, however, brings us to a higher level of development." Yet it is "disequilibrium [that] is normal and absolute whereas equilibrium is temporary and relative."[58] From this "general, objective rule" there logically follows the notion of the infinity of contradictions and struggles and the Maoist insistence that "one divides into two" is the principal law of dialectics.

Yet if these Maoist conceptions do not preclude a vision of historical progress, they do implicitly reject the Marxist vision of a historical process leading to a "total revolution" and a "final denouement" (as Marx characterized it[59]) resulting in the definitive overcoming of all contradictions and antagonisms. In the Maoist view there can be no final resolution of contradictions and no possibility of any perfect social unity. Here, it might be noted, there is a remarkable similarity between Mao and Proudhon. Like Mao, Proudhon believed that contradiction is an absolute and eternal law—although, unlike Mao, his solution was to establish an equilibrium of contradictions and antagonisms. But like Mao, Proudhon (as Robert Tucker has observed) "was opposed in principle to a search for unity in society."[60] And Proudhon's "dialectics" revolved about a notion of an everlasting distinction between the "good" and the "bad," just as Mao foresees an eternal battle between "the correct" and "the incorrect." It was, of course, precisely on these issues that Marx directed some of his most sarcastic criticisms against Proudhon. Marx accused Proudhon of failing to even pose the question of the basis of contradictions that Marx demanded be overthrown and overcome; instead, Proudhon simply accepted them as inherent in history and sought to reconcile them. Nor did Marx have a high opinion of Proudhon's understanding of dialectics: "M. Proudhon has nothing of Hegel's dialectics but the language. For him the dialectic movement is the dogmatic distinction between good and bad."[61] It would not be unfair to suggest that Marx might have viewed Mao in a similar light.

If the dystopian strain in the Maoist mentality reflects itself in projecting the contradictions and struggles of the present into the communist future (albeit in a more benign form), Mao is more profoundly dystopian in his philsophic speculations about the ultimate future of mankind. For while Mao envisions a communist future, his ultimate vision extends far beyond communism. In accordance with the dictum, first set forth in 1956, that "everything which is produced by history will also be destroyed by history,"[62] one finds "the Maoist vision" taking the following form in 1958:

> Capitalism leads to socialism, socialism leads to communism, and communist society must still be transformed, it will also have a beginning and an end . . . it cannot remain constant. . . . There is nothing in the world that does not arise, develop, and disappear. Monkeys turned into men, mankind arose; in the end, the whole human race will disappear, it may turn into something else [and] at that time the earth itself will also cease to exist. The earth must certainly be extinguished, the sun too will grow cold. . . . All things have a beginning and an end. Only two things are infinite: time and space.[63]

And again in 1964 Mao once more peered into the "post-communist" future:

> The life of dialectics is the continuous movement toward opposition. Mankind will also finally meet its doom. When theologians talk about doomsday, they are pessimistic and terrify people. We say that the end of mankind is something which will produce something more advanced than mankind. Mankind is still in its infancy.[64]

Here the Maoist "law of dialectics" is carried to its ultimate and logical absurdity.

Functions of the Maoist Vision

The general role that Maoist utopianism has played in contemporary Chinese sociohistorical development might briefly be noted, even if the more crucial questions of popular perceptions of (and mass responses to) the Maoist vision of the future are matters which remain unclear and await investigation. As is typically the case with activistic utopian mentalities, Maoism establishes a radical contrast between the

ideal and the actually existent, an extraordinary sense of
tension between a vision of what the world should be and
what it actually is, and thus serves to orient human activity
to transform the world in accordance with the ideal future
it portrays. Insofar as Maoism projects a positive Marxist
image of a socialist and communist future, it serves to give
ethical sanction to the ascetic values of struggle, self-sacrifice,
frugality, self-discipline, and hard work which are conducive
to promoting production and modern economic development
in the here and now—and the more so insofar as these familiar bourgeois virtues are presented as ultimate values and
ends in themselves. The argument that Maoism conveys
values and generates tensions which constitute a functional
equivalent to "inner-worldly asceticism" has been pursued
elsewhere and need not be belabored here.[65]

The "modernizing" role of Maoism is reinforced by the
extreme iconoclastic and strongly antitraditionalist thrust
of the doctrine. As is typical of utopian mentalities, Maoism
demands the total renunciation of the values and patterns of
behavior of the past in favor of a commitment to the new
ethics and morality of the new society it envisions: it
demands a wholesale rejection of all the values associated
with the Confucian preference for a harmonious adaptation
to the world as it is, a radical devaluation of traditional
kinship ties and particularistic loyalties, a repudiation of the
Confucian disdain for manual labor. It seeks, instead, "rational mastery over the world" and in doing so serves to encourage a spirit of experimentation and innovation favorable
to modern economic development. While the virulently
iconoclastic stance of Maoism clashes (in some respects)
with the Marxist view that the new society must be built on
the foundations of the old society from whose womb it
emerges, that socialism presupposes inheriting and appropriating all the cultural as well as material accomplishments of
the past, it is a stance well in keeping with the Weberian view
that a decisive and fundamental break with the traditions and
values of the past is an essential prerequisite for modern
economic and political rationalization. And in the tradition-

bound Chinese environment, a disciple of Weber might well view the utopian and prophetic element in Maoism as the necessary precondition to bring about that break.

Yet the Maoist utopian vision has functioned more than as simply a means of "modernization." It has had social results and political consequences largely antithetical to those posited in most theories of modernization. The messianic posture that Mao and Maoism have assumed over the past two decades has proved profoundly resistant to the development of bureaucratic professionalism and instrumental rationality, resistant to the growth of the new forms of social inequality which naturally and generally accompany the modern economic development of a backward country, and generally resistant to the institutionalization of the post-revolutionary sociopolitical order. The deeply egalitarian and antibureaucratic components of the Maoist vision, if not fully realized in social reality, have nonetheless produced a continuous (and as yet unresolved) struggle against social, political, and ideological tendencies that are incongruous with that vision of the future. If the attempts to implement the Maoist vision have not resulted in the attainment of anything resembling a classless society (or even perhaps a socialist one), they have succeeded in promoting and maintaining a remarkable degree of social equality. If bureaucracy has not (and perhaps cannot) be eliminated as Mao may wish and as his vision promises, Maoist policies have served to inhibit the stratification of bureaucratic elites operating on the basis of a vocational ethic separated from the Maoist political ethic. And perhaps most importantly, Maoist utopianism has thus far prevented the ritualization (even if not necessarily the postponement) of socialist and communist goals. The latter remain, if not realized, then at least still pursued—and twenty-five years after the establishment of Communist state power, the revolution has yet to fall victim to the presumably inevitable processes of what Robert Tucker has termed "deradicalization."[66] How long and how far this resistance to routinization and institutionalization will proceed remains of course problematic, for so much of what is unique about China's postrevolutionary history has been intimately tied to the vision and the cult of Mao, and both presuppose his person and presence.

If Mao's positive vision of a Marxist-prophesized future has served to orient human action towards achieving the economic and social goals demanded by that vision, then what is the functional significance of the dystopian strains in the Maoist mentality—the idiosyncratic vision that projects a future of endless contradictions and struggles, the vision that looks not only to a communist utopia but to the super-session of communism, a vision that foresees the end of history and the disintegration of the universe? It would seem to be the paradoxical case that Mao's dystopia plays much the same role in the contemporary world as his utopia. For the dystopian strains flow from a philosophical worldview that postulates the constancy of change as both inevitable and desirable, as both a cosmic law and a human need. It is a philosophy which teaches that change is an absolute and objective law of history and nature, and at the same time places an absolute normative value on change and the spirit of change as a way of life. Just as Mao's utopian vision of a future communist society demands human action here and now to create that society, so his long-term dystopian vision and speculations support a political and ethical demand for men to struggle and strive for change. Both his utopia and his dystopia serve to activate men to transform themselves and the world in which they live. And if Mao's ultimate vision of the dialectical movement leads out of history to the doom of mankind, to the end of time when the sun will grow cold, then that prospect lies in a future far too distant to have any imaginable relationship to the present, far too distant and unrelated to human experience to contemplate. In the meantime, Mao's dystopian philosophy conveys a message of the necessity and desirability of change in general and the ethical value of struggle to effect change in the present world.

The dystopian strain in the Maoist vision of the future—if not carried to its ultimate conclusion of the end of history and the extinction of the universe—has the perhaps paradoxical effect of making the Maoist utopia seem more historically realistic and humanly comprehensible than is generally the case with utopian visions of a future perfect order. For one of the most common and compelling objections to utopia in general is that it is a product of a sterile blueprint which portrays a society that is ultimately static, lifeless, and boring. Ralf Dahrendorf, for example, finds little difference between utopia and a cemetery, with the exception that "occasionally some things do happen in utopia." But what little happens is not very interesting because "all processes going on in utopian societies follow recurrent patterns and occur within, and as part of, the design of the whole," and thus utopia remains "a *perpetuum immobile.*"[67] The problem is that most conceptions of utopia preclude the possibility, or at least the desirability, of change. As George Kateb perceptively has observed, the problem is "the apparent incompatibility between the intention of most utopian writers and the inevitability and moral desirability of change."

> It is right to say that almost all utopian designs do not reckon with change. The common assumption is that once the design is realized in the world—if it ever is—it will continue indefinitely in the form in which it began. Utopian thought is dominated by a "rage for order." A strong utopian impetus is to save the world from as much of its confusion and disorder as possible. Utopia is a dream of order, of quiet and calm. Its background is the nightmare of history. At the same time, the order, in each case, is thought to be either perfect or as close to perfect as human affairs can get. How, in truth, could a thinker possessed both of a rage for order and a sense that he commands a vision of perfection (or near perfection) comfortably allow for change? . . . by definition, change away from perfection must necessarily be for the worse. To build in the possibility for change in utopia, therefore, is to compromise the usual premises of utopian thought.[68]

Mao, by postulating the inevitability of change and the eternity of struggle, and incorporating them into his vision of the future, has made his utopia immune to this critique.

The Maoist utopian vision not only allows for change but demands it, and at the same time envisions a future utopia which remains related to the struggles and sorrows of human experience in the present world, a future which remains fraught with risk and uncertainty and one which allows a role for human heroism and courage. Indeed, in many respects, the Maoist vision of the future fills the prescription H. G. Wells once recommended to cure utopia of its generally historically inert and humanly confining character, a prescription to create a "Modern Utopia [which] must not be static but kinetic, must shape not as a permanent state but as a hopeful stage, leading to a long ascent of stages."[69]

*Dick Howard is an associate professor of philosophy and an
adjunct professor of sociology at the State University of
New York, Stony Brook. A prolific writer, Professor
Howard's essays have been published in American, French,
and German scholarly journals and edited studies. His most
recent study,* The Marxian Legacy, *will appear in spring
1977. Among his other studies are* The Development of the
Marxian Dialectic, *and* The Unknown Dimension: European
Marxism since Lenin, *which he edited.*

5

The Future as Present:
Political and Theoretical Implications
Dick Howard

Prelude . . . and Fugue!

In retrospect, the incoherence of the New Left appears astounding. Every shade of political and moral conviction was united in single and multi-issue campaigns which brought to awareness the rent fabric in the American Joseph's coat. In an immediate sense, it was not a vision of the future but a projection and identification that united the critics—identification with guerrilla movements, be they Castroist, Christian, or Communist-Trotskyist; identification with East European intellectuals and youth, who dared speak out in the stifling world of total bureaucracy; identification with the Vietnamese, Chinese, North Koreans, and even Albanians, as well as a projection onto the American Blacks, ethnic poor, technological, and traditional working classes. Camus was as important as Marx, the Bible as "On Contradiction," Nietzsche and Freud as Bakunin and Tolstoy. All this lived comfortably (for a time) with the attempt to restructure daily life, to build a counterculture while at the same time fighting Imperialism-Capitalism as The Enemy.

Today the New Left is in such shambles, from Czechoslovakia to the Third World to our own, that we wonder what
in fact it was—dropping out, returning to God or gods, to the
earth, or to the drug-dazed sky. It is difficult to conceive of
the marches on Washington, the solidarity of the building
occupations, the intensity of the minute. When Leonard
Woodcock calls his UAW troops to Washington, it seems as
incoherent as Ford's economic experts—though perhaps
more traditional. The New Left rose like a meteor, burned
itself out, ecstatic. What happened? What traces remain?
What did it mean? Benign neglect has replaced the civil rights
movement; Allende is dead and the only "progressive"
regimes in the Third World are military; Southeast Asia is still
ablaze with U.S. complicity, while war is imminent in the
Near East; the invasion of Czechoslovakia confirmed the
most dour anticommunists; and the Lin Piao escapade,
coupled with Nixon's visit, demystified China. Unless you're
a believer in the Breakdown Theory—which the New Left
never was—it's certainly not comforting to read the economic
statistics for the U.S. today.

Because it rose so quickly and catalyzed so many hopes,
and because it died so pitifully and left nothing in its place,
the New Left presents an enigma, rich in suggestions for the
interpreter. In the context of our overall concern, the discussion of the intellectual and sociological origins, actual
practice, and implications of the New Left should prove
rewarding.

The following remarks should be read under a series of
caveats: (1) They do not claim descriptive completeness, nor
is each illustration or suggestion coupled with a stock of
references; each of us will certainly be able to provide our
own. (2) The description that is offered is conceptual and
historical at once, trying to make clear *post festum* the
choices that were often made quite unconsciously. My goal
is to offer a *framework* for a general interpretation. The
guiding thread is that the New Left was neither "necessary"
in some causal sense, nor "accidental" in an existential-
irrationalist world. It represents our society's *own self-*

interpretation. This implies a kind of reflexive sociology to whose presuppositions I can only allude in this essentially descriptive account. This over-general approach seems to have the virtue of proposing discussion, not blocking it off with "facts." (3) It has been suggested that we should take a lesson from the fact that it is not radicals who try to define radicalism; and that Marx himself has not so much a theory of revolution alongside other elements of his work, but that his entire opus is a theory of revolution—and of capitalism. Hence, I shall be less concerned with what the New Left said and/or envisioned than with what it did and the meaning of its activity for our understanding of our present situation. (4) I will be starting from the premises of Marx, adapting his method to the present, and then using the structure of that present—including the lesson of the New Left—*to criticize Marx.* This does not lessen the importance of Marx; nor should it be interpreted within a Manichean friend/foe context. I write as a participant, reflecting on the New Left experience as my own, concerned with the spirit more than the letter; and attempting here to learn something about myself and my society as well as the meaning of my—of our—work in the present. (5) This interpretation will probably please no one—a horrible way to begin a paper, but a remark that I add on rewriting. The analysis may be wrong or wrongheaded; yet I see no other approach that helps with our common problem.

Problems of Definition and of Method

If anything is clear, it is that the New Left was hardly a unified phenomenon. The term may be one of those "sponges" ridiculed by C. Wright Mills. On the other hand, it has its usefulness. It forces us to look beneath the empirical to the structural conditions which the category reflects and defines, however inadequately. It demands that we analyze in such a way that the unity and sense of our object emerge in the analysis itself. We cannot fly above our object, assuming that it has already been defined; we are looking for the *new,* and hence our method must permit it to appear.

It is not generally helpful for an historian to speak of a "New" Left in opposition to the "Old." If we were to think of the Old Left as characterized by the Leninist "party of a new type," for example, this labeling of the New Left as "New" would prove deceptive. After all, anti-Leninists of the non–Social Democratic type were strong enough to lead Lenin to write "Left-Wing Communism: An Infantile Disease," to give Stalin reason to defile and disfigure the person and work of Rosa Luxemburg, and to be partially at the root of the sacrifice of Spain to Franco and his minions—to mention but three cases that come immediately to mind.

Nor is it historically useful to distinguish a New Left from an Old Left theory of capitalism and its revolutionary potential. From the moral and liberalist utopia of the Port Huron Statement to the radical rhetoric of the Weatherpeople, Progressive Labor, and assorted company, the path was back to Marxism—but if the first time was tragedy, this time was farce as well. Encountering practical and theoretical problems —to be discussed in a moment—much of the New Left took the facile path back to "science," a kind of compensation for the "sins" of its moralistic past and a way of countering its academic enemies on their own terrain. The Marxism that was adopted was mostly of the crudest sort, mechanical in its sociology, metaphysical in its ideology. It is not surprising that, even within its own frame of reference, it made no really fruitful contributions here. As opposed to this, if we think beyond the context of the United States, the German SDS (Sozialistische Deutsche Studentenbund), for example, was probably the most scholarly political movement in recent memory, basing its new tactics and style precisely on a re-reading of Marx.[1] The same was at least partially true elsewhere, from France to Czechoslovakia.

If we try to use the criterion of "vision of the future" as a *differentia specifica,* we get only a bit further from the historical stance. If anything characterized the New Left as an everyday practice, it was its denial of a vision of the future, its insistence on living today in the everyday, incarnating the new social relations in the here and now. The "old" idea of sacrifice for the future, making the revolution for one's grandchildren, or awaiting the maturation of the contradictions, was ridiculed. This was perhaps one reason for the New Left's anti-Leninism. It certainly had something to do with the youthfulness of most of the participants; but youth is not a sufficient explanation, any more than is psychology, for a political practice.

The question of vision immediately entails that of ideology. Marxism itself of course emerged from the discovery of the function of ideology; it proceeded from an analysis of the mask of the real (critique of religion) to the analysis of the structure of the real itself (critique of capitalism). Marxists like to talk about "scientific socialism" to distinguish themselves from "utopians" of various orders. This is certainly consistent with Marx insofar as what really galled the Founder was not the goals of the utopians, but that their theory and practice hurt, not helped, the good cause.[2] But the Marxists, from Engels on, also tended to make "scientific socialism" an ideology—now in the positive sense: not just as a refutation of distinguished and misguided positions, nor solely as a guide to practice; it was also to be an ideology in the explicitly "religious," faith-giving sense. Ideology justifies the sacrifices and trials here in the capitalist present, and —however vaguely—promised the socialist future.[3]

If the Old Left had a vision of the future and an ideology —in the double sense—the New Left's immediacy and concern with the everyday today acquires a structural importance. Certainly, New Leftists threw around the term ideology and periodically were convinced that one was needed. Its lack, however, speaks loudly. Marx *discovered* ideology as a structure of the real; he did not run around accusing others of being subjectively ideologists—as his continual writing of "Critique" indicates. He did not oppose a true to a false ideology, nor a "really real" revealed by science to a false representation of it. He turned to the structure of the real in order to read its sense as ideology. The practice of the New Left is consistent with Marx's theoretical practice as ideology-critique: making the world speak the contradictory structures and imperatives which present themselves as fixed, permanent, and natural. Neither moral criticism based on values externally derived or justified, nor scientific comparison with a true and a false, a good and a bad society: Marx's theory and the New Left's practice aim, as Marx put it enigmatically in 1843, at "bringing those petrified relations to dancing by singing before them their own melody."

My methodological premise, therefore, will be that of Marx's ideology-critique: to relate the expression to the expressed, signifier to signified, in a unitary structure; to try to read the New Left as a phenomenon without prejudicing the analysis by pretending either to know the real or to know what the real ought to be. It is not a question of judging. Accepting its disparateness, refusing to privilege the "subjective" or the "objective," the attempt will be to see what the New Left has to tell us about our society and the kind of revolutionary project it engenders.

Intellectual Roots

While all the New Lefts can be understood as oriented by and around Marxism, their salient features reside in the ways in which they deviate from the model. Since the movement in the United States was the least affected by Marxism in its formative stage, these "deviant" sources expressed themselves most purely and profoundly here, and are a reason to concentrate on the U.S.

There is a further reason to concentrate on the United States. The New Left existed as a "movement," which affected far more persons than those who were organizationally affiliated with it. Its open structure permitted many to feel themselves a part of the movement, to empathize with it, and to learn from it. Particularly important to all the New Lefts were the vast protest movements that grew up in the U.S.— first the civil rights movement, then the University Reform and Free Speech Movements, and finally the movement sparked by opposition to the Vietnam War. Most striking in this *movement-character* is that the moral stance predominated over the strategic revolutionary orientation. The lack of organization of these multi-faceted movements typified also, to a large degree, the militants whose causes they supported. Particularly in the case of Vietnam, the role of *revolutionary will,* individual courage, and willingness to sacrifice, were impressive. It was inevitable that a certain *voluntarism* characterize the intellectual, organizational, political, and tactical stance of the New Left.[4]

This voluntarism which typified the climate in which the New Left functioned colored its choice of theorists. In the U.S.—though nowhere else to my knowledge—the Camus of *The Rebel* played a crucial role. Where he was replaced by Sartre, it was certainly not the Sartre of "The Communists and the Peace," nor the author of the *Critique de la raison dialectique* (only now translated after fifteen years!). Of course the existentialist tradition opened onto the anarchists on the one hand, and the mystical and self-sacrificing populists (particularly the nineteenth century Russians) on the other. Moral issues, such as those portrayed in Camus' play "The Just Assassins," dominated the discussion of means/ends—rather than the discussion of strategy and tactics, the organization question, social structure, the proletariat, and the like. When historical issues—from the Russian terrorists to the classical anarchists—arose, they were treated as part of the existential present. There was no historical consciousness, as the metaphors and images chosen by New Left writers indicate.

This existential voluntarism helps to understand the two areas where the New Left in the U.S. developed its own theoretical contribution. Psychology became important. The structural criticisms of capitalism raised, for example, in *Walden II,* made no impact: Skinner was the goat; Rogers, Fromm, and an areopagitica of pop psychologists became the common currency. Freud was not taken seriously; at best, one borrowed some rhetoric from "Civilisation and its Discontents." Wilhelm Reich came into his own only later; and even where he did—with the exception of Professor Ollman's work—it was his more idealistic side that dominated over the heavy mechanism of his "dialectical materialism." It was in this context too that Marx made his first entry: as the theorist of an ill-defined "alienation," stripped of its original connection to the structure of proletarian labor, closer to a Heideggerian fundamental ontology than to a concrete sociology. Overlaid as it was with an existential voluntarism, this psychology could immediately and easily adapt itself to the drug culture. At the same time, however, as it fled beyond, the stress also turned to the *critique of everyday life.* This theme, central to the New Left, will be treated in more detail below. For now, it is important to recognize that the turn to the (right wing) libertarianism of a Szasz, to psychiatric liberation movements, and most importantly to the small group—fundamental to the rise of the women's movement whose importance cannot be overstated—arose from an intellectual, often seemingly an antiintellectual, stance which was not arbitrary. The "getting into your own head" arose from a movement of social concern whose models of revolutionary voluntarism were consciously movements for social change. Fanon struggled with Camus, the reform of everyday life with the flight to drugs, social change with personal salvation.

The second intellectual contribution of the New Left lay, paradoxically, in the domain of the very history which the voluntarism tended to neglect: it was not History (with a capital "H") that was interesting, but the existential history of the everyday. This was typical of most of the movements. However, the United States was again unique in its choice of object. Where the Germans, for example, chose to unearth forgotten episodes and movements of their revolutionary history—the various oppositional groups during the Weimar period in particular, or the Opposition within Russia—the turn in the United States was to local history. There were of course the "revisionist" radical historians of the William Appleman Williams school and *Studies on the Left,* whose intellectual role was crucial in the debunking of myths, from the Open Door through the Progressive era down to the origins of the Cold War; there were fundamental studies like those of Felix Greene on the way we were mystified about

China;[5] and there were important attempts to revivify the specific American revolutionary tradition, from the Wobblies through the great strike movements which marked the advent of the United States as a world capitalist power. But far more important were the pioneering works on the structure of daily life—from the slave plantation to the northern city, from the gangs of the mid-nineteeth century to the relation of work and community in the twentieth century. This concern with the existential and everyday, which owed so much to the pathbreaking work of E. P. Thompson on the English working class, showed the juxtaposition of political activity with intellectual practice—and most significantly, it was conducted (for the most part) in an a-Marxist, often a-theoretical or agnostic vein. The antiintellectual stance of the New Left was not, therefore, a rejection of thought and analysis, but a questioning of a kind of Enlightenment rationality whose "dialectic" Adorno and Horkheimer had exposed years before in a little-known volume.[6]

In short, the "intellectual roots" of the New Left were largely a rejection of the traditional, rationalist views; they were part of a political practice, a social regrouping, and a personal will and moralism. None of this is the stuff of which ideologies are made, at least not politically effective ones. This was to present a problem—not a problem that arose from the material itself, nor even one that emerged necessarily from practice. The attempt was very American; very much in *our* tradition of natural law. As Jürgen Habermas has pointed out, our very moralistic natural law tradition, defended with the eloquence of a Tom Paine and the passion of Everyman, follows a Lockean notion of natural reason incarnating itself through the labor of the individual. Where the French tradition of Rousseau or the Physiocrats saw natural law rationalistically, as what ought to be—and what had to be imposed on society—the Anglo-American tradition saw it as already existing, lived in the everyday but deformed by the intervention of the state. Ours is a tradition of anarchic capitalism, of existentialists carving out their world day to day. But it is not possible to hark back explicitly to that tradition; it was smothered under its natural results: the monopolies, the consumer society, the interventionist state. Natural law anarchism was not enough. Although the Vietnamese were a model of voluntarism, they also claimed to be Marxists; so did the Chinese; and so did many participants in the movement, feeling the need for science, the passion to *make*—not just to *live*—the revolution. Marxism entered— a mysterious doctrine, sanctified, and accompanied by a priesthood, sects, and holy books. It was a disaster, a weapon in the hands of potential leaders, a cudgel to beat the individualist, and a theory for a non-theoretical movement. Of course, it was a deformed Marxism; and of course, there was much to be learned from Marx. But it came from the outside—as Lenin and Kautsky might have wished—and was not natural. The guilty adopted it, learned its rhetoric and style, or slunk away. Defining the movement atomized it; single issues became just that. The height of absurdity was reached at a California conference bringing together the black and white movements to "fight fascism." The fundamental text was Dimitrov's Speech on Fascism to the Seventh Congress of the Third International in 1935!

Social Roots

In retrospect, the introduction of Marxism as ideology into the New Left helps to clarify a fundamental feature of its development. One can look at the history of the American SDS as the search for the revolutionary subject. Not consciously at first, but ever more so, an essentially student, largely middle class group attempted to shake its guilt feelings by identifying its actions with those of the classic oppressed groups. First it was civil rights, then the liberal-labor coalition within the Democratic Party, then the various Third World peoples, and finally—and fully incoherently—a "proletariat" defined in terms of a combination of imperialism theory and Marxian orthodoxy. The history of the New Left can thus be conceived as a history of denial of self, with the resultant loss of its own originality.[7]

Marxism as ideology is not the same as a Marxian analysis

of contemporary social relations. From the latter perspective, for purposes of simplification, it might be argued that three events symbolize the changed social relations from which the New Left emerged. There was the post-1956 face lifting in Russia, whose importance is manifest not only or simply in the open "revisionism" and power politics revealed in the Sino-Soviet split, but more importantly in the consecration and open emergence of the bureaucracy as a new class operating in a new social formation.[8] Second, there was de Gaulle's assumption of power by playing off the landed and colonial capitalists against the modernizers in order to end the Algerian war and open France to a new, state-dominated capitalism.[9] Finally, there was the Kennedy tax cut, whose counterposition to Hooverian fiscal orthodoxy marked a "fiscal revolution," and symbolized a new conception of the relation of society and the state.[10] These three symbols, notwithstanding archaic remnants such as the Berlin Wall, Castro's revolution, or Sputnik, consecrate a change that restructured the globe.[11]

Broadly speaking—though the Russian case is somewhat different—the historical struggle of the working class had resulted in the paradoxical success crowned by integration into a system of countervailing powers sharing a common interest in "delivery of the goods." This class struggle operated not only through the formal mechanism of the strike; it was not always a conscious "class" struggle, and certainly not led by a party, but rather the everyday guerrilla warfare of production relations. In Marxian terms, it forced the capitalists to increase the production of relative surplus value, i.e., to introduce technological advances on an ever greater scale. At the same time, the increased intensity of labor was achieved through a variety of technical and sociopsychological means. Its results were manifold. More skills were demanded of labor-power. This meant increasing the length and quality of education, which was also necessary to prevent youthful (and other) unemployment due to the decreasing number of productive jobs. Since more and more goods were produced, an ever greater sales force of parasites was necessary, credit purchasing became the rule, and the weight of the unemployed and underemployed, as well as the ethnically underprivileged, increased; this meant in turn the increased responsibility of the state in the sphere of scientific innovation, labor training, investment credits, and social legitimation; which in turn restructured the colonial-imperial system and changed the relations of the capitalist and communist worlds. With all this arose a series of objective and subjective contradictions—between state and private capital, skilled-educated labor and routine tasks, demand for worker participation and the need to make every minute count, client and state, production and distribution, etc., as well as the tension between work and leisure, formal democracy and actual powerlessness, scientific rationalization and creative experience, education and job training, etc.

One could go on describing features; and one could debate the degree to which they are *really* differences that make a difference. The New Left's existence—though not necessarily its self-understanding—suggests a mode of analysis. Capitalism is a mode of social relations predicated on the production of surplus value and profit. It doesn't matter what is produced, nor how it is produced; to make a profit producing shoes or bibles is equivalent. Whether you accept the labor theory of value and its implications, or choose to reason commonsensically from the standpoint of the individual capitalist, the implication is that the worker is crucial to the endeavor. If the worker will work for less—longer hours or more intensively—the capitalist profits. The result is a class struggle, which manifests itself in a series of adaptations in the productive process. From being a craftsperson, whose personal skills or training are central to production, the worker becomes simply a cog. This is the classical proletariat, trained on the job, immediately replaceable, and fully dominated. Its situation is explosive; and is defused only through the formation of unions which defend its most immediate interests. Able only to "cash in," as it were, on the crisis of the 1930s and the War, this proletariat found itself restructured by the pressure that it itself put on the capitalist. Production processes changed, new technology was introduced, group dynamics were restructured. A new working class emerged. Not that the old one was eliminated or its situation altered; it is simply no longer the vanguard, the locus of struggle, the seat of felt contradictions and the source of an impulse toward the *positive* restructuring of society. The "new working class" is an ill-defined phrase, a hermeneutic device, not an empirical statistic; it suggests that capitalism develops new social needs, and that capitalism's reply to those needs points to a new structure.[12] The point is not Veblen's, Burnham's, or Galbraith's—to mention only those. It is not a permutation of an old set of relations, social goals, and norms. It is that *capitalism as a total experience changes:* its imperatives are different, its social relations modeled after a new principle, its norms in flux.

The suggestion is that captialism has changed (as has the Russian system).[13] We can begin to account for that change in terms of the class struggle and the profit imperative. But this means that, once it accounts for the new, the old theory self-destructs, so to speak. The experience of the New Left witnesses this. What was fundamental to capitalism has disappeared: the free labor market, the establishment among fully independent partners of free contracts, and the domination of production over consumption. Not that the contradictions on which it was based have disappeared, or have become less crying or cruel; exactly the opposite is true. The point, however, is that the logic of the present social conflicts is determined differently—by the logic of *bureaucratic rationality.* Such a logic is of course not foreign to classical capitalism. Weber saw its implications very early. But Weber did not go far enough in his analysis of it, and studied it in its own terms: though he knew and discussed the role of the political in the institution of bureaucratic rationality, Weber did not see that this rationality is the ultimate result not of the logic of the entrepreneur, still less of the Protestant spirit, but rather of precisely the politics of the class struggle. In a favorite Marxian metaphor, "its victory is at the same time its loss." Better, its transformation. The phenomenon of the New Left pushes us to analyze this transformation.

Tactics, Themes and Practice

The New Left considered itself a movement. Save in the phase of its ideological phantasies, it never saw itself as the expression of the proletariat; and certainly it never claimed to be a political party in any traditional sense. Its success as a movement, and its failure once it sought to limit and define itself, testifies to the correctness of this self-understanding. Given its intellectual and sociological nature, it could not have been anything else. The smoothed-over capitalism whose conflicts have shifted does not permit a frontal attack: it offends everyone, but not in the same manner. A new series of issues open, but they open in series and their unity becomes a problem. The unification which eventually poses the question of the nature of the social totality did push towards Marxism as the immediately available explanation. That didn't work. It could, and did, lead to other approaches on the level of social theory. On the level of practice, the movement form made possible a unification of the differences, however unstable and fragile.

The themes around which New Left practice centered are well known. From civil rights and antiwar through community organization, women's and gay rights, to the drug culture and student power—all of these can be unified around concern with *daily life,* and the *autonomy* of the *person.* These were lived, felt issues which demanded immediate responses. They could be communicated, it seemed, through the countermedia and the mass media. The speed at which the movement-as-feeling or attitude spread testifies to the society's ripeness. It bore witness to the homogenization of society which by covering the differences, made them all the more explosive. If the theories of the Frankfurt School, or Marcuse's writings, appeared to express the New Left, it was because of a recognition—perhaps old-fashioned in its Frankfurt formulation—of the ever-present need for autonomy in all spheres of life.

If we ask why these themes could take root as they did, the above sociological description, guided by the practice of the New Left, provides a key. Bureaucratic capitalism,

Marcuse's one-dimensional society, Adorno and Horkheimer's "dialectic of enlightenment," point to a common structure, a unity in difference: a modernity which hides itself from its own origins (analogous to the way Marx's ideology-critique in *Capital* analyzes the fetishism of commodities). The tactics of the New Left are significant in this regard: from Berkeley to Berlin, from Warsaw to Washington, and from Paris to Prague, the tactic was the deed, the confrontation, the direct action. The goal was to unmask the power relations hidden by the apparently smoothly functioning machine. The tactic unmasked the power lurking beneath bureaucratically rationalized social relations, uncovering the new structure of domination in its most intimate resting place: daily life. This tactic was not just the result of a philosophical or moral existentialism, nor the practice of desperados and outsiders; it was sociologically rooted, and pointed to the core social structure. That the New Left was able to discover this makes its experience all the more important.

The tactics, themes, and practice of the New Left reflect a further aspect of the present social structure: its use of the immediate, the here-and-now, the pseudopersonal, to cover over the root *historical* structure and *origins* of the system. "In no epoch has one talked so much," writes Claude Lefort.[14] Everything is present, open, available—from the ski vacation of "our" president to the local porn shop; from the starvation in the Sahel to the napalm in Vietnam or the Near East; from *Psychology Today* to the *Intellectual Digest*. The everyday is trivialized and thus stolen; domination is rationalized in our scientific belief systems. God is dead because we don't need her any more; we are our own gods—and hence all the more vulnerable. One can leap forward into a new whose novelty is already structurally old, vain and predictable; or one can turn to a dead past for anchorage. The system has conjured the risk of change by making change its principle. It seems to have created a closed world, a system, with no outside—Hegelianism with feedback loops.

Drawing this lesson, implicitly, the New Left committed suicide. It was incapable of imagining its own social-structural place or role, and fell back on the old models of revolution. It moved backward, groping for certainty and denying itself.

This need not have been. The stress on the immediate, on experience, on the personal, and on the communal, implicitly posed a forward-reaching demand: that of self-management, self activity, and self-representation in all spheres of life. This lesson burst forth in May 1968! No one started it; no one planned it; no one consciously wanted it. Yet it spread like a prairie fire: *l'imagination au pouvoir!* Sure, it was crushed and de Gaulle reelected; but that doesn't make it the less important. Revolutionary consciousness is not achieved overnight. The old is tenacious, the new fragile.

As an organized, self-identified movement, the New Left is dead. Its practice and its themes are still with us in communities, groups, and issues. If we turn now to some aspects of its vision, the implications of its lifestyle-as-practice, we will be able better to understand our present and its possibilities.

Implications and Questions

From its intellectual roots to its themes, tactics, and practice, the New Left represented a critique of the political. Not just a critique of politics, politicians, and the irrationality of their imperatives; the New Left rejected the political as a form of mystification—an imaginary community floating in the clouds, as Marx put it. The New Left critique of representative democracy is far more than a critique of the political from within its bounds and premises (as is the "Marxian" debunking of formal democracy, for example). It is the critique of a mode of life, a form of self and social perception. The implication is that it is in *daily life,* in "civil society," to use the consecrated term, that change must occur.

It is worth noting, however, that the apolitical politics of the New Left is a rediscovery of the path of the young Marx, from the critique of the Hegelian state through the discovery of the proletariat and the phenomenon of alienated labor. As Marx looking back at the French Revolution, so the New Left—when it looked back at all—saw that the revolution must not only destroy the political bonds that limit and narrow, but must revolutionize the sphere of personal interest and egoism. It would seem that the New Left could have followed Marx (in "On the Jewish Question") in citing Rousseau:

> Whoever dares to undertake the founding of a nation must feel himself capable of changing, so to speak, human nature and transforming each individual who is himself a complete but isolated whole into a part of something greater than himself from which he somehow derives his life and existence, substituting a limited and moral existence for physical and independent existence. Man must be deprived of his own powers and given alien powers which he cannot use without the aid of others.[15]

What emerges from the critique of the political as the constant theme and tension is, paradoxically, the *politicization* of daily life, the over-determination of every activity with a political sense, the denial of the private and the individual. As a sociological critique of contemporary bureaucratic capitalism, this stress is rich in potential. It discovered and uncovered a manifold of experience heretofore unthematized and ignored; society and socialization were experienced as a unified process, each the horizon of the other and each the critique of the other.

There was an unbearable tension in this turn to civil society and its politicization. Not simply the tension with the individualistic, existential, and anarchic roots of a movement based on moral will; the Rousseauian stress on "transforming the individual" implies a deprivation of one's "own powers," which is hardly consistent with the New Left's original impulses. Yet the internal logic of its approach drove the New Left towards Rousseau—towards Lenin and a certain Marx as well—creating a tension which would become a rupture. Activism, spontaneity, immediacy, and the lack of taboos, along with more overtly negative phenomena like antiintellectualism, drugs, and the continual strain of becoming an individual through the collective, fitted together so long as development and success did not demand reflection and analysis. With the first failures, as the movement slowed down, the poles began to separate. Society had been conceived as the relation of one to one; the future society would be one of dyadic communication; and the properly social was felt as "alienation." At the same time, however, experience pointed to the role of the *totality.* It was not simply that community organizers found that you can't create "socialism in one community," or that each single issue group found itself forced to go beyond its issue by its very successes—the demand for totalization appeared in the very immediacy of civil society, daily life, and immediate experience.

The politicization of daily life which appeared so apparent and effective a perspective implicitly implied the *destruction* of everyday life. Concern with the individual and the everyday led to the totality; but the route back remained barred. The particular and the universal were blended and collapsed, each losing what was specific to it. The psychological effects were of course disastrous. But more important here, the image of the political changed. It was through this door that a Marxian orthodoxy implicitly mediated by Lukács reentered. For all its subtlety in analyzing the phenomenon of reification in the daily existence of the proletariat, Lukács' attempt leads of necessity not simply to an *ouvrièrisme* but directly to the Leninist Party as possessor and incarnation of the totality. Though most did not read Lukács, their logic followed, or recreated, his—and returned to the old politics.

Those who remained with the original impulse of the New Left encountered another set of problems. The politicization of daily life is an attempt to remove the mystery, to render society transparent to itself, to end history in the present. This position is of course the identical obverse of the orthodox, which removes the mystery through its science, understands the present in terms of a necessary future, and sacrifices the present to that future. Making the totality, the political, present in the immediacy of daily life permitted a crtitique of that everyday experience, and guided attempts to restructure it in terms of what Trent Schroyer has called "utopian enclosures." From food co-ops to daycare centers, from small-grouping to ethnicity, the attempt was to transform the single issues into total social solutions through the transformation of the individual experience. As a form of critique-in-action, this led to an important reconsideration of the nature and role of *power* in society and social relations. At the same time, it opened a critique of the *technological rationality* of strategic action which structures our society. Here, Marcuse, Habermas, and the Frankfurt School struck the theoretical chord.

While the experiments still continue, their internal logic poses problems. On the one hand, the above considerations of the social roots of the New Left suggest that in the blabbermouth society, critique of this sort is precisely *essential* to the *masking* of social divisions. The turn to the immediate, the small group, and the closed community, naturally (not socially or politically) defined, conceals as well as reveals. It may be a personal necessity, but precisely the stress on immediacy turns it inward and limits its thrust. The identical opposite, which stresses the totality's presence in the immediate, is in fact dealing with a representation[16] of the totality which it attempts to incarnate through the creation of what Claude Lefort calls "a new social type: the militant." If you must always incarnate totality in the everyday, you *become* it, denying your particularity and your experience—and the totality is in fact lost. The quest for the totality in the immediate, whether through the dyadic group, individual consciousness, or the representational imagination of the militant, tends towards a new form of totalitarianism—which, to its credit, most of the New Left conscientiously attempted to avoid—but only at the cost of either the incoherence of its projects or the psychological integrity of its members.

The politicization of daily life is not, however, a wholly negative phenomenon: it points forward, to a redefinition of revolution and to a rethinking of the nature of society and its political structure. Explicitly, the New Left stressed and harped on two central themes, without which the notion of socialist revolution is a contradiction in terms: the end of the division of manual and mental labor, and the notion of self-management. The striving for the immediacy of dyadic communication—whatever criticism it calls forth from one standpoint—recognizes that the element of power and domination in personal relations must be eliminated. Power and domination are exercised daily in a society structured in terms of the exacerbation of the division of labor; not consciously, but of necessity, our languages are different, our self-conceptions limited, our horizons blocked, and subordination and superordination distort communication. This is ideology as the structure of our bureaucratic society. It can only be overcome with the elimination of the structured divisions which affect the individual to the core and are crystallized in that division of manual and mental labor. At the same time, the notion of self-management becomes central; it is the issue of control and power, but also that of personal relations. Self-management—not only in production but in all spheres of life—is the central theme of the New Left, essential to its vision. But the vision is not one of a future which teleologically affects practice in the present. It is a vision which bureaucratic capitalism itself calls forth, as it increasingly socializes society, making all dependent on each, and yet dividing them at work and in leisure. Self-management and the end of the division of manual and mental labor as the goal of a revolution are already inscribed as demands in our present while they are still denied in the everyday. This is why the New Left's tactics of immediate action and provocation met with such success. It seems that the success turned sour when the question of totalization emerged and, as such, either separated revolution from present activities (the Leninist view) or distorted the present by over-determining it (the group *as* future).

From this perspective, the New Left opens onto a changed sociology of contemporary society, a critique of Marxism and not simply of the simplified and vulgarized Marx of the apologists. It is obvious enough that capitalism has changed;

indeed, Marx himself can account for these changes. What is more important is that the New Left is a critique in action of Marx as the last Hegelian, of Marx the rationalist. Of course, there is the myth of the proletariat as the subject-object of history, an inverted materialist form of the Hegelian *Geist* or, politically viewed, his bureaucracy. Of greater import is the critique in action of Marx's linear view of history, of history as the progress of humanity towards its self-realization through the elimination of otherness. Capitalism is not necessarily the antechamber to the socialist reconciliation nor is it doomed to collapse through its own inner "logic." The class struggle will not come to fruition when *x* millions are unemployed, any more than revolution can be organized as a societal coup d'état. The increased role of the state, not simply as collective capitalist but as distributor of legitimation through its relation to its clients, throws into question the absolutizing of the infrastructure which is inherent in the orthodox analysis. Human relations are certainly not independent of their material substratum; but the latter is not to be taken in isolation, as the "really real" on which all else sits. Marx's analysis of laissez-faire competitive capitalism is limited to a specific case where the universe of meaning of the society is structured around accelerated reproduction through a free market—including the labor market. This was not true of precapitalist societies and only in the vaguest manner is it true today. Marx spoke of four constitutive elements of human beings: production, consciousness, language, and community. The latter three appear ever more central as liberal capitalism veers towards bureaucratic capitalism. The result is the reemergence of daily life as a sphere of contestation, and the need for a renewal of sociological analysis. Marx was not so much wrong as he was misunderstood—though the misunderstandings are inherent in the scientized self-understanding he had of his own work.[17]

The most pressing problem which emerges from the consideration of the New Left's vision is the changing role of the political. The move to civil society as the place of the

political has been seen to be paradoxical and insufficient—
or worse, to contain the seeds of a new totalitarianism. The
old politics, on the other hand, is all the more bankrupt in
that even its formal legitimacy hinged on the now-surpassed
structure of liberal capitalism. At a first level, the New Left
can be seen to reopen the domain of the political as it has
traditionally been conceived since the Greeks *invented*
democracy: as the dimension in which the good life in the
city is elaborated. Politics is neither science nor technique;
the politician is neither planner nor administrator. The slogan
of "participatory democracy" takes on its full sense here.
Politics is not the sum and substance, the totality of everyday life; it is and must remain different. At the same time,
it cannot be isolated in its difference, either determining
directly daily life from on high or being the simple addition
or representation of the atoms which compose the social.
It is the locus of power, the place where society represents
itself to itself; but at the same time that it is constitutive of
the form of the society, it is constituted by and dependent
on the society itself. Neither identical with, nor separate
from, the society, the political is not for that reason simply
nothing: it is a *process* which is unending—and whose end
could mark only the advent of a totalitarianism—in which
the society and its members seek to define and structure their
relations. In its concern with the good life of the citizens, it
is universal; in its dependence on and relation to the individuals, it is particular and open to change.

What then would revolution mean from a New Left perspective? *L'imagination au pouvoir* is not a slogan but an
analysis! Power is not to be occupied; to think that one could
—or should—seek to seize the reins of state is to be the victim
of an illusion. Axled around the demand to occupy the place
of power, revolutionary activity becomes a question of adequate means to a given end, a technological equation neglect-
ing the human material one wants to serve, and denying oneself one's own particularity. Through its experiments, however incoherent or however successful, the New Left points
to the dimension of the political process in which the good

life is put into question and developed. The forms of language, consciousness, and community take precedence over any unilateral determination of society by production and reproduction. They are the universals in terms of which the particulars structure their relations. In today's bureaucratic capitalism, the question of rationality, and with it, that of legitimation, is the locus of political debate and practice. This cannot be "seized" or "occupied," but it is nonetheless the center from which the manifold variety of empirical struggles, from the traditional workplace to the community and the classroom, spread. These latter have, and will continue to have, a surface resemblance to those predicted by the orthodox theory, but they find themselves in another context, and carry a different meaning. To treat them in the old manner would be to neglect the change, and to return to the time-worn pattern.

The implications of this "revolutionary politics" for the New Left theory are first of all found in its critique of the "Old Left." The Old Left politics—despite some glimmerings found in Marx—are caught within the bourgeois system of representation.[18] Power is conceived as a *place* to be occupied; society is seen in economic metaphors; practice is taken to be the production of an object. The goals are determined through a means/ends rationality; and success is defined in terms of a blending of theory and practice, ends and means, plan and realization. It is this *rationality* which the New Left has put into question. History is not a linear process, an empty objective space within which we move, guided by a teleological vision of the Good. The visual metaphor is destroyed; Cartesian rationalism with its "clear and distinct" ideas and causal thinking falls by the wayside, not to be replaced by an irrationalist existentialism or some qualitative physics. The process of the political is archetypical: it points to the implications of the particular in the universal, and vice versa; to the inseparability of subject and object, thought and reality, mind and body; and most importantly, it signals to us the danger of thinking that we could somehow possess the truth or totality as a thing to be held and caressed in our hands.

The New Left foundered because it was unable to recognize and realize both its own social-structural role and the implications of its critical project. It fell for the image of having (or being) the totality: either returning to an orthodoxy of Marxism-Leninism, or turning inward to the ideology of dyadic immediacy. To founder is not, however, to fail. The New Left may be dead as an organized movement—but then it never really lived as such. It lives on in all its contradictoriness because the structure of bureaucratic capitalism based on the division of society forces the emergence not only of traditional revolts, but new ones as well. If the New Left has anything to teach us, or itself to learn from its own experience, it is the dangers of objectivized "success." Perhaps the "failure" was inherent in the project; not because the project was wrongheadedly conceived, but because it can only structure itself in terms of the redefined political. The future of the New Left—its own, and the one it (however implicitly) conceived—is still with us in a project which was not engendered in the heads of the theorists, but structured into our society itself.

No explicit tactic or theory emerges from the New Left. Yet whatever we do, and however we conceive of ourselves, the structures that the New Left revealed, the imaginative tactics it applied, and its openness to experiment and self-criticism, cannot help but be of influence. This is no small tribute to its vision!

Marcus Raskin is codirector of the Institute for Policy Studies in Washington, D. C. A student of foreign policy and political philosophy, Mr. Raskin has served as a member of the Special Staff of the National Security Council under President Kennedy and the President's Panel on Educational Research from 1963 to 1965. Among his books are After 20 Years: The Decline of NATO and the Search for a New Policy in Europe *(coauthor),* The Viet-Nam Reader *(coeditor), and his provocative interpretation of American society and its relation to the state,* Being and Doing. *Mr. Raskin's most recent study,* Notes on the Old System, *is an analysis of the presidency, the state, and the Nixon period.*

6

Futurology and
Its Radical Critique

Marcus Raskin

I want to be a *Luftmensch*—a *Luftmensch* is someone who lives on air, rises and has kicks in an intellectual way. This is the way Jews used to get high. This is what makes things exciting. For many years of my life, I have been involved with the Academy [American Academy of Arts and Sciences] and teaching courses; now here is a chance to be a *Luftmensch,* to rise high and now you tell me I have to be an anchor, a ballast to drag along. I don't want to do that for a while. I want the members of the Commission to be *Luftmensch.*[1]

Governments, corporations, and social scientists believe that the control of the future can be accomplished through the development of techniques of analysis and action which assert power over how people act. Such power can be asserted through the classic means of persuasion, terror, manipulation, bribe, magic, and scientific inquiry (modes of verification) which are not readily challengeable because of their operational workability. Since the Second World War a new mode of control over the future has been developed, using methods which are epistemological hand maidens to the standard techniques—short-term policy planning, quantitative

projections, scenarios, decision theory, and simulation. These
methods are meant to show how people in their social roles
will act and interact in a future problem situation to be
structured like a setpiece military battle, with enemies and
friends alike playing their assigned parts. Certain epistemological and behavioral assumptions are shared by those who
intend to control or colonize the future. The first, and perhaps the most obvious, is the belief that organized man can
control the future, can exploit and control the world's
resources. It is not the province of God or natural determinism; it is open, to be shaped by Faustian man. In a capitalist
system the futurological assumption is that the social and
economic system will be shaped by the social scientists,
planners, etc., who are to develop the "right" kinds of institutions and forces for maintaining the system. These institutions are to be prepared by the technocratic elites away
from the people. Karl Mannheim has put it:

> Even the most radical democrat will admit to-day that in a world
> in which the work of government requires increasingly specialized
> technical knowledge and in which the most important matters are
> settled by commissions and not by the deliberations of general
> parliamentary assemblies, adequate control cannot depend on
> general approval and thorough-going publicity. Exactly the same
> holds for the various spheres of cultural life, which in the main
> require such a refined special knowledge that irresponsible chatter
> has neither controlling nor guiding value. It is very probable that
> a planned society will provide certain forms of closed social
> groups similar to our clubs, advisory councils or even sects, in
> which absolutely free discussion may take place without being
> exposed to premature and unsatisfactory criticism by the broader
> public.[2]

Leaving aside for the moment the elitist nature of those
who wish to control the future, we should note other beliefs
which are shared by the future colonizers. They believe that
there is a discernable, causal, nondialectical relationship between what people do, the consequences of their acts, and
the probable responses of others. Hence, it is unnecessary to

explain or understand people in psychological or aesthetic terms since it is assumed that they operate as objects of others, or as interchangeable units within organizations.[3] Futurology encourages the development of knowledge and facts so that prediction will result in consequential behavior. Thus, when futurologists attach themselves to corporate institutions (business, government, and military) their analysis of predictive behavior is intended to have operational consequences. To ensure the proof of the prediction the social organization is then arranged in such a manner as to fulfill the predictive prophecy. Whether reality is so mechanical or people are so malleable is beside the point—both are assumed to be by the practitioners.

Some have believed that there is both a soothsaying and prophetic quality to futurology. The question of soothsaying has always been an intensely important aspect to the psychology of palace courts. In Washington, for example, soothsaying and predicting one's future is a flourishing business conducted by palmists and soothsayers. However, the prophetic quality of futurology, that God will react to man's inequities in punishing ways if he does not reform and repent, has long since been cancelled out by the Niebuhrians, who assured us that the best we could hope for is finding means to manipulate the social structure to avoid extremes. People, things, and structure were objects of problem solving. People live "lived lives" according to forces and institutions external to the relationships they might otherwise seek, and since they have no chance to exercise any moral judgement, it is therefore unnecessary to consider a moral component. By the nature of society, they are not free and each choice is a tragically ambiguous one.

From whence did the term "futurology" derive? It was coined at the end of the Second World War by Ossip Flechtheim, and, as with Mannheim, it was meant to update the principles of positivism and the Enlightenment.[4]

According to Flechtheim the futurological approach was an attempt to discuss the evolution of man and his society in the hitherto future tense, which he said was impossible until our time. "By marshalling the ever growing resources of science and scholarship," stated Flechtheim, "we can now do more than methodically employ retrospective analysis and hypothetical predictions; we can also try to establish the degree of their credibility and probability."[5] Flechtheim's presuppositions and goals are now shared by both state socialists and American pragmatists, but each group gives its own meaning to futurology.

In a capitalist state such as the United States, futurology is predicated on a strain of deformed Hegelianism.[6] The assumption of this pseudo-Hegelianism is that classes exist in antagonism to each other. Although each class has its own consciousness, it is welded to other classes and finally mediated by bureaucratic rationalizing and a state decision-making structure. The government official, mandarin advisors, and universities are to have a supremely important task in the rationalizing process—to find a way to ameliorate class tensions and define a unifying purpose which could then be internalized in all classes. Daniel Bell and his colleagues on the Commission on the Year 2000 assumed that their ideology and spirit would become the ruling consciousness of American society. The mandarin technocratic class would share power with the capitalists and military. They believed that the exalted status to which they would transcend would also change material property relations so that the real world could fit their brand of idealism. The Commission sought to extend to the entire society goods and services which the upper classes enjoyed, to be accomplished without class struggle or economic redistribution, through technological magic practiced at the universities and implemented through the corporate industrial automation process. Bell's viewpoint was the intellectual culmination of the corporate and welfare state initiated during the New Deal. His ideas and those of the policy scientists who shared them were the fig leaves of the national security state.

Until Franklin Roosevelt, the United States prided itself on a weak federal bureaucracy and a strong civil society. However, the tenuous nature of capitalism as evidenced by the economic depression and the world thrust to war in the 1930s gave impetus to the growth of state power at the federal level. This growth did not presage an attendant change in the control of the productive process or the property relations in the society. Indeed, principles of planning were introduced to sustain the capitalist class structure and the nation-state. After the Second World War the state bureaucracy was organized around three principles—the ideology of anticommunism, the cultural imperative of "firstness," and the economic trajectory of growth and expansion to avoid class struggle.

Since the society had developed great schisms during the economic depression, the question remained for established power as to whether the three principles could be burned into the consciousness and daily life of people so that the manifestly different interests which the various classes had could be neutralized. It was believed by planners that with these three principles the differences between the classes could be harmonized through orderly growth and change which would appear to be "obviously" rational to all in the society.

Whether in the Department of Defense, the corporation, or the city, it was assumed—and still is—that there is a knowledge for obtaining this harmony: the knowledge learned in policy planning, futurology, and the policy sciences, the knowledge of manipulation. Conscious or not, such colonizing knowledge justifies the transformation of communities into markets to sell and places to conquer. It is a mode of manipulated social change to be governed from the top. After all, who could better use and implement the results of decision theory: a general or a soldier, a corporate owner or a worker, a government leader or a citizen of the city?

Anticommunism became an ideal and a driving force. Men and women who in their youth supported or flirted with communism now continued the totalization process by assuming that all reality was the communist reality: it was only whether one was for or against it. The practical consequences of the anticommunist ideal were war preparation, interventionary and continuous military engagement. American democracy in the service of capitalist principles tried to pretend that democracy and monopoly capitalism are inextricably linked. The power and stability of the state were directly related to its ability to reach beyond the daily concerns of people and put them in touch with Crusades and war activities meant to overcome the boredom and humdrum of modern life. John Kennedy attempted to develop a set of heroic and sacrificial myths which would overcome this void. Intellectuals whose task it has been to develop the "music" for the great institutions and the great crusades have accompanied their deformed Hegelianism with a belief in unconnected empirical facts.

Futurology, however, is an attenuated form of positivism in three ways. First, the empirical social fact is utilized in the way facts are supposedly used in the natural sciences, namely, that the only datum is the *res extensa*—that which can be empirically observed (thus excluding potentiality and consciousness). Second, quantitative methods of the social sciences take precedence over other methods and stress the relativism of truth. As Robert Merton and Daniel Lerner said in 1951: "We do not take into account 'personal' motivations, such as love of truth or an appetite for knowledge, since there do not exist valid data on this matter and since it is practically impossible to assign to them today even an approximate place on a calibrated scale of national distribution."[7] Third, instrumental needs of different classes and individuals were to be held together by a spirit transcending the "ordinary" cares and by obvious manipulations through the most powerful forces of the society. John Dewey and James Tufts pointed to the problems involved when they said at the beginning of the twentieth century that, from the ethical point of view, the democratic ideal poses rather than solves the great problem of how to harmonize the development of each individual with the maintenance of a social state in which the activities of one will contribute to the good of all the others. It also expresses a postulate in the sense of a demand to be realized: that each individual will have the opportunity for release, expression, and fulfillment of his distinctive capacities, and that the outcome will further the establishment of a fund of shared values.[8]

These ideas were made practical at the end of the Second World War by the American pragmatists who invented "policy sciences." The postwar period encouraged answers to Marxism and its political call for comprehensive transformation. The American problem solvers sought an ideology which would not only eschew existential weariness and revolutionary turbulence but also one which would befit American imperial responsibilities. *It would have to be an ideology which would reject ideology.* Harold Lasswell, for example, stated that the method of the policy sciences was not political. He believed that politics was irrational, corrupt, and "anti-scientific." The words of the method were technocratic and neutral, supposedly reflecting a mode of thought which could not be challenged. The researcher's motivations were also taken to be beyond question. It was the consequence (and in some instances the intention) of the policy sciences to avoid the question whether social science had its own interests, class bias, or hidden agenda of political practice. According to Harold Lasswell, the policy sciences could speak for everyone. Their technocratic mode would start as the "dominant current among many scholars and scientists notably in the social sciences" and then move "more specifically toward the policy sciences of democracy."[9] Apparently what Marxism was supposed to be (but was not) to the socialist state, the policy sciences would be to democracy.

Planning was the staple for policy making. According to Charles Rothwell, planning was a "systematic attempt to shape the future. When such planning becomes a prelude to action, it is policy making. For policy, broadly speaking, is a body of principles to guide action."[10] It is calculated choice to (1) clarify goals, (2) develop means to choose between "options," (3) estimate in some form of quantitative way probable consequences of alternative directions, and (4) determine the "optimum means for carrying out the action decided upon." This mode of thought spoke to a whole generation of technocrats who lived in one reality, in one situation, and spent their days planning another one, either for themselves or for others. They believed in problem solving, which came to mean the application of instrumental rationality to particular situations which would paper over class difference and avoid class conflict. The policy sciences, planning and futurology, became the philosophical pragmatist's practical tool to forget about the past, unless it could be used instrumentally to control the future. Man was to be judged not by his unique qualities but by scientific principles, which meant that he would be able to be molded and directed. Organized and large-scale institutions totalized the life of people so that there was no escape from the process which somehow was thought to be rational.

The historical precursors to policy planning and futurology were gentle and serious men. They were not *danse macabrists* like Herman Kahn who enjoyed titillating audiences with the need for nuclear weapons and then clucking about the consequent horror they would bring when used. Indeed, social science meant something quite different to the pragmatist precursors. As Robert Lynd pointed out, knowledge was to be man's instrument for salvation.[11] The pragmatists and the Marxists were the children of the Enlightenment. Unfortunately, embedded in the Enlightenment position was the modern scientific imperial lesson that man is at war with nature. It was generally believed by scientists and imperialists alike that a dualistic tension existed between man and nature. Very few understood that the domination of nature as an ideology and practice would also have to mean the domination of man. The slow, the "primitive," the communal, and tactile, those who saw their culture as part of nature would have to give up their animism to the totemic rationality of the modern world.[12] Ethics became an instrument of problem solving and a means of justifying actions. There were no standards of history or standards anterior or invariant to the situation or moment which were called upon as guides.

The intellectual worker of the government, corporations, and military has been *debased* into constructing "as if" worlds for the present colonizing institutions. In the "as if" world the work of the intellectual worker, Daniel Bell's *Luftmensch,* is reduced to contingency plans for tactical nuclear wars in Europe, laying out eight alternative world visions, forecasting the number of cars General Motors can sell in the year 2000. In the "as if" world there is no history of people. There is no existential or cultural importance to the past. There is a radical elimination of history. Instead, there is a history of the future.

"As if" bureaucracies have a task beyond self-preservation and status acquisition—they too must predict and control the future, and they must also find a way to routinize the Faustian spirit. While its members live comfortable but alienated lives, their reason for existence is to overcome obstacles and solve problems. The Faustian bureaucrats and futurologists saw life as a series of conflicts to overcome with their slide rules, military force, and admonitions about too much growth and not enough growth. They came to believe that their plans—antiseptic but rational in a calculative sense —could be accomplished through the hierarchy of power, as it exists. They believed like good Weberian bureaucrats that they would not have to get involved in politics, in a system of exchanges, or in existential risks that a person would have to make if he were political. For them there is no sense of personal despair. As the Faustian bureaucrats plan the way whole populations are treated, human behavior is further channelized, mediated through assigned social roles which are objectified and routinized. The Faustian "as if" world supposedly becomes more predictable, and people are characterized into "as if" ways of acting which are then quantitatively measured. Such measurements are invariably one dimensional projections of frozen facts arrived at by quantitative means or one dimensional fantasies (scenarios).

Neither the induced facts through social channelization nor the fantasy of the scenario tells us what the facts relate to and what is the underlying reality of human behavior. Just as discrete behavioral facts are limited because they do not explain the underlying reality or the social motion, so "as if" forecasting is also hobbled because it is based on observed behavioral phenomena which say nothing about the inner life of the person. It describes behaviors to which the person is reduced, or induced to follow. (It should be noted in passing that the new bureaucratic class is given over to "finding out" every crevice of a person's life or a group's interactive life. The information gathered, whether by schools, police, or credit bureaus, is used to track and arrange the person's existence. This process of investigation might be referred to as *profilism.* Profilism does not allow people to be judged by their unique qualities nor does it develop institutional models which begin from principles of uniqueness.) This form of thinking is ripped out of the anthropological and philosophic knowledge of history, law, and therapeutic psychology since the reduction of a person to behavior or to a measurable unit does not take account of a person's subjectivity—his being—or the social situation in which he finds himself. No judgements are made and major social facts and organizations which employ such thought remain hidden. It is of no factual interest that the draftee in the Indo-China war is not in the jungle by his choice, that the levels of categorization laid onto children for future channeling are not their choice, or that the decisions of the Open Market Committee of the Federal Reserve System which controls the money supply are not the choice of the workers.[13]

By planning for the future on the basis of existing social organization, its attendant class structure, colonizing technology, and knowledge, we are robbing people of their future, of what they are, outside of faulty superstructures. We are robbing them, as well, of their potentiality. As Max Horkheimer in the *Eclipse of Reason* has said:

> Just as all life tends today increasingly to be subjected to rationalization and planning, so the life of each individual including his own hidden impulses which formerly constituted his private domain must now take the demands of rationalization and planning into account. The individual's self-preservation presupposes his adjustment to the requirements of the preservation of the system, a system, by the way, which is undefined and no one quite knows in fact what it is. And just as the process of ration-

alization is no longer the result of the anonymous forces of the market but is decided in the consciousness of a planning minority, so the mass of subjects must deliberately adjust themselves, the subject must so to speak devote all his energies to being in and of the movement of "things."[14]

In other words, he is required to mediate his reality through the things that appear out there, through, if you like, the consumer goods which exist, the police, the military, and the banking system. The faulty social system is not seen as the problem. It is the people who must internalize the idea that they are the problematic, the potentially or perpetually guilty ones who are to be sacrificed or used. Yet as I think about this kind of bureaucratic Faustianism, I am struck by the fact that it is quite petty. It asserts a tragedy to human existence which can only be corrected by elites and technologies from the top and does not see faulty superstructures in a state of stinking decay as the reason for our present situation. These studies, which now lead scholars to talk about how to sacrifice millions of people whether through war or famine or pharaonic planning, purvey the deformations and agonies of the people.

Commission reports are neither projects of liberation nor art. Whereas in 1966 the best intentions of American imperial concern was reflected in the Commission on the Year 2000, a few years later the futurologists were developing "lifeboat strategies" which would maintain profligacy and faulty superstructure. This mood was quickly picked up in the media and now reflects the thrust of the bourgeois doomsayers. It is not hard to determine what the cause was of the change in this attitude—the loss of the war in Indo-China, plus reliance on world resources for America's wasteful economic system, caused the mandarins to rethink their own rosy predictions for the future. The assumptions of the Commission were related to technocratic efficiency, a do-goodness, and its mandarin predominance. While the attempt at rationalization remained present, an ethics of self-preservation took hold. The language of the futurists also changed dramatically to a certitude and determinism which was missing from the less strident musings of the 1960s.

Press reports carried stories of futurologists who said that we must plan for the inevitable disaster of overpopulation and depleted resources. One of the proponents of this point of view, Dr. Garrett Hardin, professor of human ecology at the University of California, Santa Barbara, developed the charming little metaphor: "Suppose a ship sinks and there are a thousand people swimming for their lives—but only one lifeboat. It is filled to capacity, perhaps will hold five or ten more people if they are jammed in. But eventually a point is reached at which the lifeboat will sink if one more person struggles to climb aboard. Those who have managed to get aboard face the terrible and agonizing task of pushing away the others, who are doomed."[15] This point of view, found in varying forms among the middle class academics on the West Coast and members of the liberal intelligentsia, reflects a pervasive fear that decline has occurred and disaster is now the nature of American existence, including their own. It stems from the present shaky condition of the American empire and the loss of Indo-China. It has caused the mandarins to reassess the ground upon which they present their theories and to throw over any ethical pretense of community or sharing through production.

The artist long ago understood the emptiness and desperation of state and corporate plans. The great novels of dystopia, *1984* and *Brave New World,* started from a fundamental insight. They asserted that planning for the future through organizational and hierarchical means (the state, party, or corporation) when accompanied by a science without moral purpose, in fact destroyed the inner truth and the quest for justice—those very impulses which have given impetus to the cultural and political revolutions of the twentieth century. These books, which damned power and rationalization, showed the reader a vision of bourgeois and state socialist one-dimensionality which smothered man's internal and external space. Huxley and Orwell, children of the British middle class, that very class which was so committed to merely observable behavior, concluded that all of modern life was nothing more than surface phenomena, trivia, and horror. They seemed to be saying that the corporate and bureaucratic planners, the advocates of scientism, were without understanding of man's internal life, his internal structure, where moral truths and the spirit of justice are formed. How could anyone comprehend the material life which was necessary to sustain the aspirations of people if the internal truths of people were denied? This question cannot be answered by capitalism (even though it tries) with its frozen pyramidal art at Lincoln Center or its advertising extravaganzas meant to blot out local cultures in favor of national and international prepackaged foods and ideas.

On the eve of the Second World War, Archibald MacLeish pleaded it was only the poet who could help us understand and transform the future.

> The economists . . . cannot help us. Mathematicians of the mob, their function is to tell us what, as a mob, we have done. . . . When they try to build their theories out beyond the past, ahead of history, they will build like wasps with paper. And for this reason: their laws come after, not before, the act of human wishing, and the human wish to live in and make true. For what is lacking in the crises of our times is only this: the image. Its absence is the crisis. It is the act of the spirit which fails in us. With no means or with very few, men who could imagine a common good have created great civilizations. With every means, with every wealth, men who are incapable of imagining a common good create ruin. This failure of the spirit is a failure from which only poetry can deliver us.[16]

Beyond being a craftsman who makes the furniture of our senses and minds, the artist also comprehends the inner life. It is in this realm that those who construct "as if" fantasies are so lacking. Plato, who in the *Republic* fails to understand the inner life except as wishes to be repressed, is aware, however, that the poet-artist is a public expression of the inner life. The Platonic understanding "gave dramatic and poetic expression at once to the demonstration that the poet, inspired by divinity or madness, perceives truths and achieves values not otherwise accessible to man."[17]

Through his work, the literary artist, for example, relates prudentiality to moral content. The artist knows that prudentiality is the major social value which limits Faustian greed. If man's behavior was caused by fortune outside his control, it was considered either the price for having left Eden or the playfulness of the gods. On the other hand, if he tried to dictate to fortune or to those forces which could neither be seen nor understood the man was thought to be a tragic and dangerous figure, much like Oedipus. He was driven and imprudent.

Besides comprehending the value of limits, art informs the political culture because it reflects a

> profound expression of the aspirations and interests of the people in a given historical stage, and as such it maintains a certain relationship with politics. This relationship is neither external, imposed from without, nor direct and immediate. Because of this relationship, the work of art is tendentious, and in this sense, as Engels wrote in his letter to Minna Kautsky on November 26, 1885, all great art is tendentious. "The father of tragedy, Aeschylus, and the father of comedy, Aristophanes, were both powerfully tendentious poets, as were Dante and Cervantes, and the main merit of Schiller's *Cunning and Love* is that it is the first German political tendentious drama."[18]

To be concerned with radical social reconstruction means understanding the difference between facts and truth. It is a difference that artists intuitively understand. Bureaucracies manufacture facts, but they cannot find a way of dealing with truth. The artist gives dramatic and poetic expression to the divinity or the sense of madness or the perception of truth which the rest of us are somehow afraid to confront or bring into the open. The artist is someone who says what wants to be said. It is unmediated and therefore it is dislocating, and *obvious.*

The artist begins by asserting that truth is within us and beyond social systems. It is expressed myths which are not time-bound and which repeat themselves in many guises in the history of man's culture. The same elements are always present. Thus, if one wanted to understand the past and the future he could undertake to master myth. Through myth existential truths are discovered about reality. On the other hand, modern love of calculative thinking has meant that we are not clear on what is real or what is reality. As I have suggested, calculative thinking translates the qualities and substance of the world into numerical representations. But such representations are shields against understanding the things and processes themselves. Richard McKeon, in praising Thomas Mann, claimed that it was the artist who understood the nature of myth and truths which were *there* beneath numbers and calculations: "We have lost our sense of the profundities of truth because we have confused truths with facts that we can see and feel and test by their utility, and we have come to suspect the myth, because we suppose literal-mindedly that, unlike history, the myth did not happen and therefore is not true."[19] (The problem is that we have not understood the question of utility—for whom, for what—which the artist and possibly the philosopher can formulate in the struggle for community.)

We would be wrong to think of scenarios conjured at think tanks as myths which teach fundamental truths. While they usually deal with how leaders will act, scenarios do not set forth invariant principles of human nature, but rather describe organizationally how people who have one particular role will act if they are mechanical and bloodless. Rather than "disciplining the imagination" as Herman Kahn says, the person now mixes together reality and fantasy partaking of the zany qualities of Hollywood which packages "as if" reality and fantasy to the point where Americans describe reality by saying that "it's just like in the movies."

The problem with the scenario is that is also ripped out of time, geography, tradition, and psychology. It is deformed structuralism which assumes that, like money and numbers, countries and people are interchangeable. If a particular scenario prediction does not apply to France, it might apply to Italy. As Herman Kahn has said, the problems "might look very different from those abstract problems actually predicted for the hypothetical France of 1975 since both 'predictions,' the actual ones about France and the hypothetical

ones by a non-existent supremely competent planner, are
necessarily abstracted from reality."[20] The problems of inter-
changeability, of using information and ideas ripped out of
their original context, universalizes ideas which should have
only limited meaning or specific objectives. Their inventors
refuse to recognize their limited nature. Consequently, state
bureaucracies revolve around permanent "threat situations,"
and defense is seen as "taking out" cities of millions of
people wherever they may be or holding hostage millions,
whether French, Russian, Chinese, or American. In other
words, judgement about ideas is lost because ideas are ripped
from human passion.

The scenario is an attempt to take man's need to imitate,
to act, and to play, and use that fundamental aesthetic impulse in relation to problems of war and power. In one sense
the perverted use of an art form defeats what art forms teach
us: that there are unique human acts—"The anguish of death,
desire, love, the faith that makes the believer or militant
revolutionary joyfully accept sacrifice, the emotion felt at
the beauty of nature or of a human being all remain irredu-
cible to concepts."[21] They can neither be explained through
utilitarian language charts, etc., nor can they be play-acted except as a farce. Even as farce Stanley Kubrick's *Dr. Strange-
love* teaches us more about nuclear reality than Herman
Kahn's *On Thermonuclear War* because Kubrick depicts our
needs and desires, our personhood beyond social role.
Kubrick's farce deals with passions and, as Bertrand Russell
has said, it is human passion which defines the moral content
of a person's actions. Imaginary intellectual ("as if") games
are aimed at denying human passions. This play activity is a
softening-up process for genocide. Paul Goodman has pointed
out that bureaucracies develop format language to cover their
activities.

> Format is Speech colonized, broken-spirited. It is a use of speech
> as social cement, but it is not like the small talk of acquaintances
> on the street in their spontaneous style; it is a collective style for
> a mass. . . . Diplomats, administrators of all kinds, and other
> public relators, who have to make remarks about what is none of

our business, have always used a style to drain meaning from what they say. . . . The government of a complicated modern society cannot lie much. But by format, even without trying, it can kill feeling, memory, learning, observation, imagination, logic, grammar, or any other faculty of free writing.[22]

When the reader or listener is privileged to appraise the works of Henry Kissinger we witness the master of format language, just as Robert McNamara and Dean Rusk are masters of format language, just as proposals for government grants and foundation grants require such format language. But worse, this language is now the nonreferential and untruthful crutch which allows us to develop an insane highway system, or terrible schools, or an economic system that has lost sight of any life or human purpose.

The question of aesthetics is integral to the consideration of methodology and the future. The development, for example, of accidental or chance music now presents us with a new insight. It is no longer the task of music to communicate truth or structures which are beyond themselves. It is enough to be. The structure of the music becomes, like a dance, a statement of one's own persona. Communication remains meaningful only if it is concrete. "Music is just *there*, and any analytical celebrations only interfere with its experience as a primary fact. Art and nature thus merge into one: there is no qualitative experiential distinction between listening to the sound of music and the noise of nature."[23] Thus, the purpose of new music is to emphasize the improvisatory and unique qualities of the listeners and the sense experience. It becomes a unique moment which is not intended to be replicated. In this process the transcendent is achieved because the limits of language are overcome through the arts. Roger Garaudy has wondered whether it is not time to reaffirm the rights of "Dionysus the dancer against Apollo the sculptor and artisan. Is not Zorba the Greek a saint for our time who shows us that there are crucial things that only dance can express?"[24] I raise this question of aesthetics and music for several reasons. One is that it holds inner truths for people. The project, for example, of jazz improvisation, shows us how each person can be related and involved with another using chance, knowledge, skill, and an audience which is unashamed of itself, each waiting and together guessing the next note, the next moment. Is this not the basic workings of a democratic community?

Once we reject futurology and point out the importance and timeliness of art as an expression of the people's needs, of where they want and *need* to go, there will no doubt be those who will assume that I am saying that art causes politics to vanish much in the manner that Lasswell hoped that policy sciences would be beyond politics or dogmatic Marxists believe that scientific administration takes the place of politics once social classes disappear. Both art and politics are man's natural condition. Today we are involved in the historic process of developing a politics of transformation. Such a politics is a constant process, beyond assigned role or planner's model which seeks to take each transitory moment and develop from it a sustained dynamic of radical reconstruction. Art, on the other hand, besides being timely in the political sense, is timeless in the impulses expressed and the works made. It "outlives its own time and continues to live in harmony with the movement of real life itself. . . . Inasmuch as art is an affirmation, expression, and objectification of man, understood in a concrete way as a social and historical being, art sinks its roots in that profound and authentic vein of humanity, the people."[25]

Gramsci's interpretation of art as profound aspiration of people in any particular historical period means that once we recognize unconquered art we can understand the aspirations which people crave.[26] This craving we may call the principle of negativity. People are saying that the principle of stopping, and then transforming, social institutions which attempt to colonize the people's time and space is now a crucial political and necessary human task. This may be accomplished in many ways. Clearly, one of them is to reconsider the deal which Faust made with Mephistopheles (the relationship of knowledge to power). In less metaphorical terms it is clear that the science of genetics, of life itself, is the study of limits, structures, and essences. These are the questions from which we cannot escape. Nor can we escape confronting capitalism and deformed socialism. The fashion today is to reopen the question of planning. Obviously, planning is merely the reflection of the balance of social forces at any one time. John Dewey had hoped for a different kind of planning than has emerged in the world. He pointed out that there was an immense difference between the planned society and the continuously planning society.[27] The former requires blueprints imposed from above and therefore involving reliance upon physical and psychological force to secure conformity to them. The latter means the release of intelligence through the widest form of cooperative give and take. The attempt to plan social organization without the freest possible play of intelligence contradicts the very idea in social planning. For the latter is an operative method of activity, not a predetermined set of final truths. Perhaps if we can agree on the principle of negativity, of recognizing Zorba the Greek, the fact of human limits (*vir est natus ab utero et faecis*) we can move to radical reconstruction through continuous "social planning" and participation of the people.

Once we recognize the obvious, the need for negativity and therefore the development of space for an alternative, we will be able to see the outlines of a new society.

Notes

Notes to Chapter Two

1. See Harold J. Massingham, *The Golden Age* (New York: William Morrow, 1928).

2. I have dealt with this in detail in Nisbet, *Social Change and History* (New York: Oxford University Press, 1969), chaps. 3, 4, and 5.

3. See Robert Nisbet, "Turgot and the Contexts of Progress," *Proceedings of the American Philosophical Society* 119, no. 3 (June 1975): 214-222.

4. See Frederick J. Teggart, ed., *The Idea of Progress: A Collection of Readings* (Berkeley: University of California Press, 1929). Also Nisbet, *Social Change and History.*

5. Marie J. Condorcet, *Sketch for a Historical Picture of the Progress of the Human Mind,* trans. June Barraclough (London: Weidenfeld and Nicolson, 1955), p. 4.

6. Ibid., p. 199.

7. Guenter Lewy, *Religion and Revolution* (New York: Oxford University Press, 1974), chap. 6.

8. Crane Brinton, *The Jacobins* (New York: Russell and Russell, 1961). See also Robert R. Palmer, *Twelve Who Ruled* (Princeton, N. J.: Princeton University Press, 1941), pp. 322-324.

9. Palmer, *Twelve Who Ruled,* p. 324. See also Robert R. Palmer, *The Age of Democratic Revolution* (Princeton, N. J.: Princeton University Press, 1964), vol. 2, *The Struggle,* pp. 127-128.

10. Quoted in Palmer, *The Struggle,* pp. 242-243.

11. See Nisbet, *Social Change and History,* chap. 5; also Frederick J. Teggart, *Theory of History* (New Haven, Conn.: Yale University Press, 1925), chap. 11.

12. See Robert Nisbet, *The Social Philosophers* (New York: Thomas Y. Crowell, 1973), pp. 221-247

13. Raymond Williams, *Culture and Society: 1780-1950* (Garden City, N. Y.: Doubleday, 1960), pp. xi-xvi. Also Eric Hobsbawm, *The Age of Revolution: Europe 1789-1848* (New York: Mentor Books, 1964), p. 17.

14. See *The Positive Philosophy of Auguste Comte,* trans. Harriet Martineau (London: G. Bell & Sons, 1896), vol. 1, chaps. 1 and 2.

15. Beginning with Edmund Burke's strictures on the combined democracy, equalitarianism, centralization, and also economism of the French Revolution, in his *Reflections on the Revolution in France* and continuing through the writings of the French conservatives, Maistre, Bonald, and Chateaubriand, the English Coleridge and Southey, the German Haller and Hegel, and the Spanish Donoso y Cortés and Balmes, on down through Carlyle, Arnold, Tocqueville, Taine, and others of traditionalist bent, we find by all odds the most devastating treatments of political and economic modernity in this "reactionary" tradition. As George Bernard Shaw once wrote, Marx, by comparison with John Ruskin, is virtually a member of the Manchester School. It was in their evocation of the values of the precapitalist, predemocratic period that the conservatives launched their attack.

16. See Massingham, *Golden Age,* pp. 50-59. Also Margaret T. Hodgen, *The Doctrine of Survivals* (London: Allenson & Co., 1936).

17. Hodgen, *Doctrine of Survivals,* especially chap. 1.

18. This point is commonly overlooked in those histories of social thought in which the distinction is made sharply between the "utopian" and the "scientific" radical thinkers of the nineteenth century, with Marx inevitably made to lead the procession of the latter. The fact is, so-called utopians from Saint-Simon on set their visions of the future in laws of development which were for them just as "iron" as Marx's were. The great difference between the utopias of such writers as More, Bacon, and Campanella, in the sixteenth century, and the utopias of the nineteenth century is that whereas the former were, and were intended to be, no more than imaginative pictures of alternative societies, the latter were regarded by their authors—Saint-Simon, Comte, Fourier, Marx *et al.*—as "necessary" outcomes of historical-

developmental processes. This is why nineteenth century utopian thought is so often associated with authoritarian, even terroristic, modes of thinking. It is, after all, one thing to oppose or to disagree with a mere model that has been set forth; it is something very different to be guilty of willfully opposing what has been shown to be the development—the progress!—of mankind.

19. It was on this point that anarchists and Marxists—really from the disagreement in Paris between Marx and Proudhon onward—disagreed so strongly in the nineteenth century, and continue to disagree to the present moment. Marx's vision in the final pages of the *Manifesto* of the centralization necessary during the first stages of the impending revolution, of the stages which would take place within "the vast association of the nation" and, later, his insistence upon the "revolutionary dictatorship of the proletariat," together with Engels' defense, after Marx's death, of the kind of discipline that is inherent, he said, in the factory, all of this inevitably made Proudhon, Bakunin, and their disciples suspicious of Marxist words on freedom and the withering away of the state. Anarchist disillusionment with the Russian Revolution of 1917 was, of course, early.

20. Cited in J. B. Bury, *The Idea of Progress* (London: Macmillan & Co., 1920), p. 282.

21. "Letters of Henri de Saint-Simon to an American," in *Selected Writings,* ed. and trans. F. M. H. Markham (Oxford: Blackwell, 1952), p. 70.

22. Ibid., pp. 69-70.

23. See especially Saint-Simon's *New Christianity* in *Selected Writings,* Markham. See also Emile Durkheim, *Socialism and Saint-Simon* (New York: Collier, 1952); and Frank E. Manuel, *The New World of Saint-Simon* (Cambridge, Mass.: Harvard University Press, 1956).

24. See especially Fourier, *Le Nouveau Monde Industriel et Sociétaire* (Paris: Bossange, 1829).

25. Robert Hine, *California's Utopian Colonies* (San Marino, Calif.: Huntington Library, 1953).

26. Marx's letter was written to Engels and can be found in his *Selected Correspondence.* It is well known to all students of Marx, but, for obvious reasons, not often referred to by Marxists themselves. Marx and Engels were both fascinated by war, its strategy and tactics, and well aware of the dependence of modern warfare upon total organization of political, economic, and social resources in populations waging war.

Sigmund Neumann, in his "Engels and Marx: Military Concepts of the Social Revolutionaries," in *Makers of Modern Strategy*, ed. Edward Mead Earle (Princeton, N. J.: Princeton University Press, 1943), correctly, in my judgement, places Marx and Engels among "the fathers of modern total war." Lenin's endorsement of national wars—to the profound disagreement of contemporary pacifist socialists—on the ground that national wars could be converted into civil wars would, I am morally certain, have earned praise from both Marx and Engels. It is worth adding here that Marx and Engels followed the course of the American Civil War with utmost interest and also sophistication.

27. *Selected Writings of P.-J. Proudhon*, ed. Stewart Edwards, trans. Elizabeth Fraser (Garden City, N. Y.: Doubleday Anchor, 1969), p. 246.

28. Ibid., p. 239.

29. Ibid., p. 245.

30. See Robert Nisbet, "DeBonald and the Concept of the Social Group," *Journal of the History of Ideas* 5, no. 3 (June 1944):315-331.

31. *Selected Writings of P.-J. Proudhon*, p. 92.

32. Ibid.

33. Ibid., p. 244.

34. See Georges Sorel, *Illusions of Progress*, ed. John Stanley, trans. Charlotte Stanley, with Foreword by Robert Nisbet (Berkeley: University of California Press, 1969).

35. On Sorel's thought see Richard D. Humphrey, *Georges Sorel: Prophet without Honor* (Cambridge, Mass.: Harvard University Press, 1951); and Irving L. Horowitz, *Radicalism and the Revolt against Reason: The Social Theories of Georges Sorel* (London: Routledge, 1961).

36. Georges Sorel, *Reflections on Violence*, trans. T. E. Hulme and J. Roth (London: Collier-Macmillan, 1961), pp. 123-124.

Notes to Chapter Three

1. Herbert Marcuse, *Five Lectures: Psychoanalysis, Politics and Utopia*, trans. Jeremy J. Shapiro and Shierry M. Weber (Boston: Beacon Press, 1970), p. 62.

2. Karl Marx, "Letter to Ruge," in *Writings of the Young Marx on*

Philosophy and Society, trans. and ed. Loyd D. Easton and Kurt H. Guddat (Garden City, N. Y.: Doubleday Press, 1967), p. 212.

3. Though Marx considered revolution the most likely possibility, he lists England, the United States, and Holland as countries where socialism might be attained by "peaceful means." Hans Gerth, ed., *The First International: Minutes of the Hague Congress of 1872* (Madison: University of Wisconsin Press, 1958), p. 236.

4. Karl Marx and Friedrich Engels. *German Ideology,* trans. R. Pascal (London: Laurence & Wishart, 1942), p. 26. Engels, in a letter written shortly before his death, goes so far as to say that it is impossible to provide details on communism "without falling into utopianism or empty phrasemaking." Karl Marx and Friedrich Engels, *Werke* (Berlin: Dietz, 1968), vol. 39, p. 195. Such a view of attempts to describe the future was also a part of Marx's Hegelian heritage. Hegel had said, "Since philosophy is the exploration of the rational, it is for that reason the apprehension of the present and actual, not the erection of a beyond, supposed to exist, God knows where, or rather which exists, and we can perfectly well say where, namely in the error of a one-sided, empty ratiocination." G. W. F. Hegel, *Philosophy of Right,* trans. T. M. Knox (Oxford: The Clarendon Press, 1942), p. 10.

5. Karl Marx and Friedrich Engels, *Briefwechsel* (Berlin: Dietz, 1949), vol. 1, p. 348.

6. Karl Marx, "Critique of the Gotha Program," *Selected Writings,* (Moscow: Foreign Languages Publishing House, 1951), vol. 2, p. 21.

7. Ibid., p. 21.

8. Karl Marx and Friedrich Engels, *Communist Manifesto,* trans. Samuel Moore (Chicago: H. Regnery Co., 1955), pp. 55-56.

9. Marx, "Civil War in France," in *Selected Writings,* vol. 1, p. 476.

10. H. Meyer, "Marx on Bakunin," *Etudes de Marxologie* 91 (October 1956):108-109.

11. Ibid., p. 109.

12. Marx, "Civil War," p. 476.

13. Marx, "Gotha Critique," p. 22.

14. Karl Marx, Friedrich Engels, et al., "Forderungen der Kommunistischen Partei in Deutschland," *Werke* (Berlin: Dietz, 1959), vol. 5, pp. 58-68.

15. According to Marx, capitalism created a "vast number of employments, at present indispensable, but in themselves superfluous."

Advertising, insurance, and the stock exchange are obvious cases of "industries" which would disappear in what Marx calls "the avoidance of all useless labor." Karl Marx, *Capital,* trans. S. Moore and E. Aveling (Moscow: Foreign Languages Publishing House, 1958), vol. 1, p. 530.

16. Marx, Engels, et al., "Forderungen der Kommunistischen Partei," p. 4.

17. Marx, *Capital* (Moscow: Foreign Languages Publishing House, 1959), vol. 3, p. 826.

18. Marx, "Civil War," p. 474; "Gotha Critique," p. 22.

19. Marx and Engels, *German Ideology,* p. 44. Marx goes on to explain that "the town, is in actual fact the concentration of the population, of the instruments of production, of capital, of pleasures, of needs, while the country demonstrates just the opposite fact, their isolation and separation."

20. Marx, *Capital,* vol. 3, p. 793; *Communist Manifesto,* p. 18.

21. Marx and Engels, *German Ideology,* p. 44.

22. Marx, *Capital,* vol. 1, p. 505.

23. Marx, "Gotha Critique," p. 32.

24. John Bellers, a seventeenth century English writer, is allowed to express their common view on this subject: "An idle learning being little better than the learning of idleness. . . . Bodily labor, it's a primitive institution of God. . . . Labor being as proper for the body's health as eating is for its living; for what pains a man saves by ease, he will find in disease. . . . Labor adds oil to the lamp of life, when thinking inflames it. . . . A childish silly employ . . . leaves the children's minds silly." Marx, *Capital,* vol. 1, pp. 488-489.

25. Ibid., p. 484. He also says that "technical instruction, both theoretical and practical, will take its proper place in working class schools." Ibid., p. 488.

26. H. Draper, "Marx and the Dictatorship of the Proletariat," *Etudes de Marxologie* 129 (September, 1962):30.

27. Marx, Engels, et al., "Weltgesellschaft der Revolutionären Kommunisten," *Werke* (Berlin, Dietz: 1960), vol. 7, p. 553.

28. Meyer, "Marx on Bakunin," p. 108.

29. Marx, "Civil War," p. 473.

30. Ibid., p. 471.

31. Ibid.

32. Ibid., pp. 470, 471.

33. Ibid., p. 472.

34. Meyer, "Marx on Bakunin," p. 112.

35. Marx and Engels, *German Ideology*, p. 25.

36. Marx, *Capital*, vol. 3, p. 86. Marx strongly approved of the factory laws passed by the Paris Commune. Marx, "Civil War," p. 478.

37. Marx, *Capital*, vol. 1, p. 530.

38. Marx, *Theorien über der Mehrwert*, ed. K. Kautsky (Stuttgart: J. H. Dietz, 1905–1910), vol. 3, pp. 303-304.

39. Marx, *Capital*, vol. 1, p. 530.

40. Marx, *Capital*, vol, 3, p. 854; Marx, *Poverty of Philosophy* (Moscow: Foreign Languages Publishing House, n.d.), p. 70.

41. Marx, *Capital*, vol. 3, p. 184.

42. Marx, "Gotha Critique," p. 20.

43. Ibid., pp. 20-21.

44. Marx, "Civil War," p. 471.

45. Marx, *Capital*, vol. 1, p. 530.

46. Marx says, "What the producer is deprived of in his capacity as a private individual benefits him . . . in his capacity as a member of the society." Marx, "Gotha Critique," p. 21.

47. Ibid., pp. 21-22.

48. Marx, "Civil War," p. 471.

49. Marx, *Capital*, vol. 2, p. 358.

50. Marx, "Gotha Critique," p. 22.

51. For an interesting debate between those who see extensive workers' control operating at this time and those who believe Marx favors centralized state ownership and control of industry, see the articles by R. Selucky and H. H. Ticktin in *Critique* 3 (Autumn 1974). Marx's actual comments on this subject make it difficult to come out strongly for either view.

52. Marx, *Poverty of Philosophy*, p. 161.

53. Marx, "Gotha Critique," p. 23.

54. Marx, *Economic and Philosophic Manuscripts of 1844*, trans. M. Milligan (Moscow: Foreign Languages Publishing House, 1959), pp. 111-112.

55. Marx and Engels, *German Ideology*, p. 22.

56. In communism, work is "not only a means of life, but life's prime want." Marx, "Gotha Critique," p. 23.

57. Marx and Engels, *Deutsche Ideologie*, in *Werke* (Berlin: Dietz, 1961), vol. 3, p. 378.

58. Marx approvingly quotes Hegel that, "By well educated men we understand in the first instance, those who can do everything others can do." Marx, *Capital*, vol. 1, p. 363. I hasten to add that for Marx this includes much more than it does for Hegel. This statement was not quoted by Marx for the purpose to which it is being used here, but I consider the inference to communist education a legitimate one.

59. Marx and Engels, *Deutsche Ideologie*, p. 378.

60. Marx and Engels, *German Ideology*, p. 189; Marx, "Gotha Critique," p. 22.

61. This marvelous versatility of communist man is generally taken for granted by Marx; he never presents us with a brief. In his works, however, he gives several instances from his own time which are meant to indicate the festival of talents to come. Marx tells us that "the workers, in their communist propaganda, affirm that it is the vocation, the destination of each man to develop himself in many different ways, to realize all his dispositions, including the ability to think." Marx and Engels, *Deutsche Ideologie*, p. 273. Marx opposes this claim to Stirner's view that to strive for such multifaceted development is foreign to man's nature. And even in capitalist society, when extraordinary conditions allow it, individuals surprise themselves and contemporaries with their capacity for varied work. Marx quotes a French worker of his day who writes, after returning from a stay in the New World, "I never could have believed, that I was capable of working at the various occupations I was employed on in California. I was firmly convinced that I was fit for nothing but letter-press printing. . . . Once in the midst of this world of adventurers, who change their occupation as often as they do their shirt, egad, I did as the others. As mining did not turn out remunerative enough, I left it for the town, where in succession I became a typographer, slater, plumber, etc. In consequence of thus finding out that I am fit for any sort of work, I feel less of a mollusk and more of a man." Marx, *Capital*, vol. 1, p. 487. In the ideal conditions of communism, this sense of accomplishment would be far greater and would apply to everybody.

62. Marx, *1844 Manuscripts*, p. 104.

63. Ibid.

64. Marx and Engels, *German Ideology,* p. 27.

65. It is in this sense, that Marx declares, "Society . . . is man himself in his social relations," and "not until man has recognized his own capacities as social capacities . . . will human emancipation be a-chieved." Marx, *Grundrisse der Kritik der Politischen Ökonomie* (Berlin: Dietz, 1953), p. 600; Marx and Engels, *Werke,* vol. 1, p. 370.

66. Marx claims that in production, "the labor power of all the different individuals is consciously applied as the combined labor power of the community." Marx, *Capital,* vol. 1, p. 78.

67. On one occasion, this recognition is expressed as follows: "You are placed in a human relation with my product, you have need of my product. This exists for you then as an object of your desire and of your will." Marx and Engels, *Gesamtausgabe,* ed. V. Adoratsky (Berlin: 1932), vol. 1, part 3, p. 544.

68. Ibid., pp. 546-547. Marx continues, "I would also have the job of having been for you the mediator between you and the human species, therefore of being recognized and experienced by you yourself as a complement of your own nature and as a necessary part of your being, therefore of knowing myself affirmed in your thoughts as in your love. Finally, the joy of having produced in the individual manifestation of my life the direct manifestation of your life, therefore of having af-firmed and realized in my individual activity my true nature, my human nature, my social being." And, again, "In so far as man, and hence also his feelings, etc., are human, the affirmation of the objects by another is likewise his own enjoyment." *1844 Manuscripts,* p. 136. This idea is also expressed in the claim that, "Need or enjoyment have consequently lost their egotistical nature." Ibid., p. 107.

69. Marx and Engels, *Gesamtausgabe,* vol. 1, part 3, p. 547.

70. Marx gives us some indication of what this is like in a passage where he describes socialist workers of his own time and the new need they have acquired for "society": "what appears as a means becomes an end. You can observe this practical process in its most splendid results wherever you can see French socialist workers together. Such things as smoking, drinking, eating, etc., are no longer means of contact or means that bring together. Company, association, conversation, which again has society as its end, are enough for them." Marx, *1844 Manuscripts,* p. 124. The tendencies of an advanced section of workers in capitalism are firmly and fully established among everyone in communism.

71. Marx and Engels, *Communist Manifesto,* p. 36.

72. Marx, *1844 Manuscripts,* p. 102.

73. Ibid., p. 107.

74. Marx, *Capital*, vol. 3, p. 757.

75. Ibid., p. 854.

76. Marx, "Gotha Critique," p. 23. A typical criticism of this principle which shows how far most commentators are from grasping the people and conditions of communism is O. D. Skelton's claim that the individual's desire is unlimited, and if he himself decides his needs, "the socialist treasury would be bankrupt in a week." Yet, he claims, if there is an official estimate, the opportunities for tyranny and graft are enormous. O. D. Skelton, *Socialism* (Boston: Houghton Mifflin, 1911), p. 203.

77. Marx and Engels, *Deutsche Ideologie*, p. 424.

78. Marx and Engels, *German Ideology*, p. 68.

79. Marx, *Capital*, vol. 1, p. 75. Marx is quoting here from Engels' early essay, "Outlines of a Critique of Political Economy."

80. Marx, *1844 Manuscripts*, p. 111.

81. Marx, *Grundrisse*, p. 440.

82. Marx and Engels, *German Ideology*, p. 70.

83. Ibid.

84. Marx, *1844 Manuscripts*, p. 104. Thus, too, Marx can declare that "communism as fully developed naturalism equals humanism," and that "it is the genuine resolution of the conflict between man and nature." Ibid., p. 102.

85. Marx and Engels, *Deutsche Ideologie*, p. 411.

86. Marx and Engels, *German Ideology*, p. 18.

87. Ibid., p. 75.

88. Marx, *Capital*, vol. 3, p. 376.

89. Marx and Engels, *Communist Manifesto*, p. 36.

90. Marx, "Gotha Critique," p. 23.

91. Marx, *Capital*, vol. 3, p. 83.

92. Marx, *Grundrisse*, p. 505.

93. Marx, *Capital*, vol. 3, pp. 799-800.

94. Marx and Engels, *The Holy Family*, trans. R. Dixon (Moscow: Foreign Languages Publishing House, 1956), p. 176.

95. Marx, *Grundrisse*, p. 505. Marx also says, "Really free labor . . .

gives up its purely natural, primitive aspects and becomes the activity of a subject controlling all the forces of nature in the productive process." Ibid.

96. Marx and Engels, *On Colonialism* (Moscow: Foreign Languages Publishing House, n.d.), p. 52.

97. Marx, *Capital*, vol. 3, p. 799.

98. Marx and Engels, *Holy Family*, p. 238.

99. Ibid., p. 239.

100. Marx and Engels, *Communist Manifesto*, p. 43. *"Assoziierten Individuen"* has been seriously mistranslated in the English editions of the *Manifesto* as "a vast association of the whole *nation*" (as opposed to "of associated *individuals*"), lending a statist tone to this popular quotation which it does not have. I am thankful to Peter Bergman for pointing this out to me.

101. Marx, "Gotha Critique," p. 30.

102. Marx and Engels, *On Colonialism*, p. 126.

103. Meyer, "Marx on Bakunin," p. 112.

104. Marx and Engels, *Communist Manifesto*, p. 39.

105. Marx and Engels, *Deutsche Ideologie*, p. 378.

106. Ibid., p. 411.

107. Marx and Engels, *German Ideology*, p. 27.

108. Marx, "Gotha Critique," p. 22.

109. Marx and Engels, *German Ideology*, p. 44.

110. Marx, "Gotha Critique," p. 22.

111. Meyer, "Marx on Bakunin," p. 108.

112. For a fuller treatment of class, see my article, "Marx's Use of 'Class,' " *American Journal of Sociology* 5 (March 1968):573-580.

113. Marx and Engels, *Deutsche Ideologie*, p. 410.

114. Marx, "Thesis on Feuerbach," in *German Ideology*, p. 198.

115. Marx and Engels, *Communist Manifesto*, pp. 37-39.

116. Ibid., p. 37.

117. He says, "The setting up of a communal domestic economy presupposes the development of machinery, of the use of natural forces and of many other productive forces—for example of water-supplies, of gas-lighting, steam-heating, etc., the removal of the antagonism of town and

country. Without these conditions a communal economy would not in itself form a new productive force; lacking any material basis and rest- on a purely theoretical foundation, it would be a mere freak and would end in nothing more than a monastic economy. What was possible can be seen in the formation of towns and the erection of communal buildings for various definite purposes (prisons, barracks, etc.). That the abolition of individual economy is inseparable from the abolition of the family is self-evident." Marx and Engels, *German Ideology,* pp. 17-18.

118. Marx and Engels, *Communist Manifesto,* pp. 38-39.

119. Marx, *1844 Manuscripts,* pp. 99-100.

120. Ibid., p. 141.

121. Marx and Engels, *The Holy Family.* Cecily, Rigollette, and Fleur de Marie are the positive characters in the novel for Marx.

122. Marx, *1844 Manuscripts,* pp. 100-101.

123. The tempting though dangerous comparison between the commu- nist version of the family and the Israeli *kibbutz* may have crossed the minds of some readers. Though people living in *kibbutzim* exercise considerable primary democracy, eat in communal dining halls, share some household tasks, and raise their children in common, I find the comparison dangerously misleading for the following reasons: (1) The *kibbutz* operates in an economy of scarcity, which necessitates that women work, that people eat in a communal dining hall, that children are raised in common, etc. This gives a Spartan character to all these activities which is decidedly noncommunist. (2) The *kibbutz* is set in the countryside, which setting and its accompanying mode of existence is glorified in a sort of Tolstoyan agrarian mystique; as a result, its inhabitants have too little contact with city work, technology, and culture, all of which reflect on family relationships. (3) The *kibbutz* exists in a specific state, Israel, and must abide by the laws of that state in all matters relating to marriage, divorce, children, etc. This is a straitjacket that communist man does not wear. (4) The *kibbutz* has too many restrictive rules for family life as for all else, especially when compared to a society which has none. (5) Finally, people living on the *kibbutz,* like all other groups in the world today, are of another genre than the people of communism. The same activity or form of organization becomes something else when the people involved act from widely varying motives, achieve other kinds of satisfaction, under- stand their actions differently, and so on.

124. Marx says that in communism the evolution of species man finally

coincides with the evolution of each particular individual. Marx, *Theorien über Mehrwert,* ed. K. Kautsky (Stuttgart: Dietz, 1921), vol. 2, p. 309.

125. Marx, *1844 Manuscripts,* pp. 101, 105, 151.

126. For an account of capitalism which stresses the internal relations between all its components, see my book, *Alienation: Marx's Conception of Man in Capitalist Society* (Cambridge, Mass.: Cambridge University Press, 1971).

127. Ibid., parts 2 and 3.

128. A final word on the sources of Marx's vision of communism: having as my main purpose to reconstruct this vision and believing that it is internally related to Marx's analysis of capitalism, I have purposely omitted all mention of the Utopian socialists. Yet, there is no question but that Fourier, Saint-Simon, and Owen in particular, exercised an important influence on Marx. They have been left out of this paper because I distinguish between those ideas which brought Marx to that analysis of capitalism and history we call "Marxism" and the somewhat similar views which exist as a part of this analysis. The Utopians' vision of the future, operating as some kind of ethical ideal because it stands outside of what is understood of man and society, contributed to Marx's early political stance and clearly influenced the direction of his studies. Once Marx's analysis reached the point where he could project the real possibilities inherent in capitalist society, however, the logical status of such views changed from being the independent principle or ideal in an ethical system to being an integral (if still to be realized) part of the real world. The same analysis resulting in a sifting and refocusing of whatever notions Marx inherited on communism in line with newly discovered possibilities. Lacking such an analysis, the Utopians could only serve up a mixture of dreams, intuitions, and fond hopes. If it is necessary to study the Utopians, therefore, in order to understand how Marx came to Marxism, including its vision of the future, the same study may actually distort what these ideas are and confuse rather than help our efforts to judge them.

Other useful discussions of Marx's vision of communism can be found in Ralf Dahrendorf, *Marx in Perspektive* (Hanover: 1953), particularly pp. 72-117; Thilo Ramm, "Die Künftige Gesellschaftsordnung nach der Theorie von Marx und Engels," in *Marxismusstudien,* ed. Irving Fetscher (Tübingen: J. B. Mohr, 1957), pp. 77-119; Jean Yves Calvez, *La Pensée de Karl Marx* (Paris: Editions du Seuil, 1956), pp. 504-554; Kostas Axelos, *Marx penseur de la technique* (Paris: Les Editions de Minuit, 1970), part 5; and the various articles in

Etudes de Marxologie 4, no. 11 (November 1970). For the fullest selection of Marx's comments on communism, see Maximilien Rubel, ed., *Pages choisies pour une éthique socialiste* (Paris: 1948). The extent to which Russian Marxists and their Western followers have pared down Marx's vision can be seen from the articles in *Recherches internationales à la lumière du Marxisme*, vol. 18, *Le Communisme: Aujourd'hui et demain* (Paris: Editions de la Nouvelle Critique, 1960).

Notes to Chapter Four

1. Lewis Mumford, *The Story of Utopias* (New York: Viking Press, 1962), p. 1.

2. Norman Cohn, *The Pursuit of the Millennium* (New York: Harper & Row, 1961), pp. 308-309.

3. J. L. Talmon, *The Origins of Totalitarian Democracy* (New York: Praeger, 1965), pp. 252-253.

4. Adam Ulam, "Socialism and Utopia," *Daedalus* (Spring 1965):392.

5. Ibid., p. 399.

6. As G. Pettee has observed: "From the time of the American and French Revolutions to about 1940 it would seem fair to say that the general opinion in the West was that revolution is good when needed, and that the conditions in which it is needed can occur fairly often. There were voices to the contrary, of course, but they were at least seemingly outnumbered. From about 1940 on, there has been slowly increasing doubt of this belief. . . . The supporters of revolution are now little heard in the advanced West. The great concern is with countermeasures to revolution as an instrument of power politics, and with the means by which states and governments may be brought along most quickly and effectively to make revolution unnecessary. There is a strong emphasis on military strength as the immediate means of defending the existing regimes; and also considerable awareness that this may be overemphasis. But there is much agreement that revolution should be prevented or forestalled." Cited in Carl Friedrich, ed., *Revolution* (New York: Atherton Press, 1967), pp. 29-30.

7. See for example, Frank E. Manuel, ed., *Utopias and Utopian Thought* (Boston: Beacon Press, 1967); George Kateb, *Utopia and Its Enemies* (New York: Free Press of Glencoe, 1963); and Frederik Polak, *The Image of the Future* (Dobbs Ferry, N. Y.: Oceana Publishers, 1961).

8. Karl Mannheim, *Ideology and Utopia* (New York: Harcourt Brace, 1952), p. 173.

9. Ibid., pp. 173-179.

10. Max Weber, *The Sociology of Religion* (Boston: Beacon Press, 1963), p. 144.

11. Ibid., especially pp. 95-117.

12. Peter Worsley, *The Trumpet Shall Sound*, second augmented edition (New York: Shocken Books, 1968), p. xiii.

13. Ibid, p. xiv. For an excellent and enlightening discussion of this and related theoretical problems which cannot be considered adequately here, see Worsley's introduction to the second edition of *The Trumpet Shall Sound*, pp. ix-lxix.

14. Reinhard Bendix, *Max Weber: An Intellectual Portrait* (Garden City, N. Y.: Doubleday, 1962), p. 259. While it is true that in his introduction Worsley perhaps defines the problem more precisely and treats it more clearly than did Weber, his criticism that Weber concentrated on the personality of the prophet to the neglect of the more crucial question of the nature of the relationship between leaders and followers is perhaps better directed at some of Weber's latter-day disciples than Weber himself. Indeed, the problem of how "the inspirations of a few become the convictions of the many" is one of the principal questions raised by Weber. Whether "Weberians" have dealt with the question in adequate fashion is quite another matter.

15. Frederik L. Polak, "Utopia and Cultural Renewal," in *Utopias and Utopian Thought*, p. 288.

16. Mannheim, *Ideology and Utopia*, p. 236.

17. From *Max Weber: Essays in Sociology*, eds. Hans Gerth and C. Wright Mills (New York: Oxford University Press, 1958), p. 128.

18. Talmon, *Origins of Totalitarian Democracy.*

19. As characterized by Waldemar Gurian, "Totalitarianism as Political Religion," in *Totalitarianism*, ed. Carl J. Friedrich (New York: Grosset & Dunlap, 1964), pp. 119-137. The theme is pursued by Gurian in *Bolshevism: An Introduction to Soviet Communism* (Notre Dame, Ind.: University of Notre Dame Press, 1952).

20. Carl J. Friedrich, "The Unique Character of Totalitarian Society," in *Totalitarianism*, p. 52.

21. Michael Walzer, *The Revolution of the Saints* (Cambridge, Mass.: Harvard University Press, 1965), pp. viii-ix.

22. *Times* (London), 25 July 1938.

23. Mao Tse-tung, "On People's Democratic Dictatorship" (July 1949), in *Selected Works of Mao Tse-tung* (Peking: Foreign Languages Press, 1961), vol. 4, especially pp. 411-412 and 418-422.

24. Mao Tse-tung, "Report of an Investigation into the Peasant Movement in Hunan" (March 1927), *Selected Works of Mao Tse-tung* (London: Lawrence & Wishart, 1954), vol. 1, p. 22.

25. Mao Tse-tung, "The Question of Agricultural Cooperation" (31 July 1955), in *Communist China 1955-1959: Policy Documents with Analysis,* eds. Robert Bowie and John K. Fairbank (Cambridge, Mass.: Harvard University Press, 1962).

26. Mao Tse-tung, "On the Ten Great Relationships" (25 April 1956), translated in *Mao Tse-tung Unrehearsed, Talks and Letters 1956-71,* ed. Stuart Schram (London: Penguin Books, 1974), pp. 61-83 (hereafter referred to as *Mao Unrehearsed*).

27. "Resolution on Questions Concerning People's Communes" (Delivered at the Sixth Plenary Session of the Eighth Committee of the Chinese Communist Party, 10 December 1958). Reprinted by *New China News Agency* (Peking), 18 December 1958.

28. "The integration of the *hsiang* with the commune," it was typically proclaimed, "will make the commune not very different from the Paris Commune, integrating the economic organization with the organization of state power." See Wu Chih-pu, "On People's Communes," *Chung-kuo ch'ing-nien pao* [China youth] , 16 September 1958.

29. "Apart from their other characteristics, China's 600,000,000 people have two remarkable peculiarities: they are first of all, poor, and secondly blank. This may seem like a bad thing, but it is really a good thing. Poor people want change, want to do things, want revolution. A clean sheet of paper has no blotches, and so the newest and most beautiful pictures can be painted on it." *Hung-ch'i* [Red flag] , 1 June 1958, pp. 3-4.

30. Mao Tse-tung, "Sixty Points on Working Methods" (19 February 1958), translated in *Mao Papers,* ed. Jerome Cohen (London: Oxford University Press, 1970), p. 66.

31. Ibid., p. 65.

32. Mao Tse-tung, "Speech at the Lushan Conference" (23 July 1959), in *Mao Unrehearsed,* pp. 145-146.

33. Ibid., p. 139.

34. Mao Tse-tung, "Talk at an Enlarged Central Work Conference" (30 January 1962), in ibid., pp. 170-173.

35. Ibid., p. 175.

36. Ibid., pp. 174-175.

37. Ibid., p. 168.

38. Mao Tse-tung, "Speech at the Tenth Plenum of the Eighth Central Committee" (24 September 1962), in ibid., p. 189.

39. Mao Tse-tung, "Speech at the Enlarged Session of the Military Affairs Committee and the External Affairs Conference" (11 September 1959), in ibid., p. 149.

40. See Mao Tse-tung, "Report to the Second Plenary Session of the Seventh Central Committee of the Communist Party of China," in *Selected Works of Mao Tse-tung* (Peking: Foreign Languages Press, 1961), vol. 4, p. 374.

41. Mao Tse-tung, "Talk at the First Plenum of the Ninth Central Committee of the Chinese Communist Party" (28 April 1969), in *Mao Unrehearsed*, p. 288.

42. For a brief discussion, see Maurice Meisner, "Leninism and Maoism: Some Populist Perspectives on Marxism-Leninism in China," *China Quarterly* 45 (January–March 1971):17.

43. *Mao Tse-tung Ssu-hsiang Wan-sui* [Long Live Mao Tse-tung Thought] (Taipei, 1969), pp. 333-334.

44. Mao Tse-tung, "Talks at Chengtu" (22 March 1958) in *Mao Unrehearsed*, pp. 118-119.

45. Mao Tse-tung, "Remarks at the Spring Festival" (13 February 1964), in ibid., p. 204.

46. Mao, "Talks at Chengtu," in ibid., pp. 119-120.

47. Mao, "Remarks at the Spring Festival," in ibid., p. 207.

48. Ibid., pp. 210-211.

49. Mao, "Speech at the Lushan Conference," in ibid., p. 140.

50. The enormous Maoist extollation of popular folk culture—what Mao in the Yenan years praised as "the fine old culture of the people which has a more or less democratic and revolutionary character"—stands of course in striking contrast to the iconoclastic Maoist attitude toward both the Chinese Confucian tradition and the Western tradition. See Mao Tse-tung, *On New Democracy* (Peking: Foreign Languages Press, 1940).

51. Mao Tse-tung, "On Contradictions," in *Selected Works of Mao Tse-tung* (London: Lawrence & Wishart, 1954), vol. 2, pp. 51-52.

52. Mao, "On the Ten Great Relationships," in *Mao Unrehearsed,* p. 81.

53. Mao Tse-tung, *On the Correct Handling of Contradictions among the People* (Peking: Foreign Language Press, 1957), p. 51.

54. Mao, "Sixty Points on Working Methods," in *Mao Papers,* p. 65.

55. Ibid.

56. "Summary of Chairman Mao's Talks with Responsible Comrades during His Provincial Tour" (August–September 1971), in *Mao Unrehearsed,* pp. 297-298.

57. Mao Tse-tung, "Talk at Seventh Plenum of the Eighth Central Committee of the Chinese Communist Party," translated in "Miscellany of Mao Tse-tung Thought (1949-1968)," *Joint Publications Research Service* 61269–1 (Springfield, Va.: National Technical Information Service, 1974), p. 175.

58. Mao, "Sixty Points on Working Methods," in *Mao Papers,* p. 66.

59. Karl Marx, *The Poverty of Philosophy* (Moscow: Foreign Languages Publishing House, n.d.), p. 168.

60. Robert C. Tucker, "Marx and Distributive Justice," in *The Marxian Revolutionary Idea,* ed. Robert Tucker (New York: Norton, 1969), p. 52.

61. Marx, *The Poverty of Philosophy,* p. 108.

62. Mao, "On the Ten Great Relationships," in *Mao Unrehearsed,* p. 75.

63. Mao, "Talks at Chengtu," in ibid., p. 110.

64. Mao Tse-tung, "Talk on Questions of Philosophy," in ibid., p. 228.

65. See Maurice Meisner, "Utopian Goals and Ascetic Values in Chinese Communist Ideology," *Journal of Asian Studies* 28, no. 1 (November 1968):101-110.

66. See Robert C. Tucker, "The Deradicalization of Marxist Movements," in *Marxian Revolutionary Idea,* pp. 172-214.

67. Ralf Dahrendorf, "Out of Utopia: Toward a Reorientation of Sociological Analysis," in *Utopia,* ed. George Kateb (New York: Atherton Press, 1971), p. 106.

68. *Utopia,* p. 8.

69. H. G. Wells, *A Modern Utopia* (1905), quoted in *Utopia,* p. 9.

Notes to Chapter Five

1. For example, the early SDS leaders and their present-day heirs engaged in detailed rereadings of Marx. See, for example, Michael Mauke, *Die Klassentheorie von Marx und Engels* (Frankfurt: Europäische Verlagsanstalt, 1970); Oskar Negt, "Marxismus als Legitimationswissenschaft," introduction to Abram Deborin and Nikolai Bucharin, *Kontroversen über dialektischen und mechanistischen Materialismus* (Frankfurt: Suhrkamp, 1969); and Hans-Jürgen Krahl's work on the *Grundrisse*, in *Konstitution und Klassenkampf* (Frankfurt: Verl. Neue Kritik, 1971). Recent work in Germany has concentrated itself around what amounts sometimes to a "Marx philology with revolutionary intent," reinterpreting the "logic" and the "dialectic" of *Capital*.

2. On Marx's attitude to the utopians, see the fundamental reexamination by Miguel Abensour, "L'histoire de l'utopie et le destin de sa critique," in *Textures* (Belgium), 73:6-7 and 74:8-9. Abensour stresses a "new utopian spirit."

3. An example is found in a 1912 sociological survey: A 29-year-old metal worker states, "I am not without hope, for one who is so filled with socialism as myself believes in a liberation like a new Gospel." Or a 39-year-old metal worker, who states that "It was the political and trade-union movement which first gave a goal to my being, a content to my life." Citations from Helga Grebing, *Geschichte der deutschen Arbeiterbewegung* (Munich: Nymphenburger Verlagshandlung, 1966). One could cite Dietzgen, Engels, Gramsci, and many others to similar effect.

4. A possible third reason for concentrating on the United States—its position as leader of the capitalist world, where presumably the contradictions, cooptations, etc., are most advanced—is questionable. Particularly as concerns the role of the state, one could look to the examples of France, Britain, or Scandinavia as models. This is not the place to debate which country is the "vanguard of capitalism."

5. Felix Greene, *A Curtain of Ignorance* (Garden City, N. Y.: Doubleday, 1964).

6. Max Horkheimer and Theodor Adorno, *Dialectics of Enlightenment* (New York: Herter and Herter, 1972).

7. This is not to propose a psychologizing interpretation, or to suggest the correlative reductionism. The argument is sociological, posed in terms of social structure and the nature of sociality, as will be seen. It helps to explain the mess in which the remnants of the New Left find

themselves—from Jesus freaks to gurus, to the resurging "Leninist" sects, to the withdrawal into drugs and/or communal ventures.

8. Cf. the lucid analysis by Claude Lefort, "Le Totalitarisme sans Staline," first published in *Socialisme ou Barbarie* 14 (1956); now in his *Eléments d'une critique de la bureaucratie* (Geneva–Paris: Droz, 1971).

9. See the analysis of Paul Cardan (Cornelius Castoriadis) in *Socialisme ou Barbarie;* as well as those of Serge Mallet in *Le Gaullisme et la gauche* (Paris: Editions du Seuil, 1965).

10. The term is taken from the title of Herbert Stein's useful work, *The Fiscal Revolution in America* (Chicago: University of Chicago Press, 1969). The analysis, of course, differs from his.

11. I omit references to the Chinese Revolution and its aftermath, and to the succession of ex-colonies assuming independence in one or another manner. Not that these are unimportant; simply that their symbolic dimensions can only be understood in the mirror of the productivized, bureaucratic capitalist countries.

12. On the "new working class" theory and its implications, see Serge Mallet, *The New Working Class: A Socialist Perspective,* ed. and trans. Dick Howard and Dean Savage (St. Louis, Mo.: Telos Press, 1976). Mallet provides a specific illustration of his thesis through an analysis of French capitalism.

13. Marx predicts this in the form of state capitalism. Simply, Marx didn't see its implications for the structure of the wage-labor/capital relation, and expected the old contradictions to persist in an unchanged manner. This is not the case, and explains the error of "state capitalism" theses which propose to explain Russia through a kind of Marx-reading. In the former case, that of capitalism, one must recognize that the political sphere has changed its locus, and that the economic class struggle is no longer the central pivot of the system. One would be led, then, to analyses similar to—but not identical with—those of J. Habermas' recent *Legitimation Problems of Late Capitalism* (Boston: Beacon Press, 1976). In the latter case, one could not suggest that the Party is simply a collective capitalist, against whom the workers must organize, as before, and struggle from the workplace. To this (more or less Trotskyist) approach, one would have to oppose an analysis of the political over-determination of social life which, as Castoriadis and Lefort have argued, makes of the Russian situation *a historically-new social formation.* On this latter, cf. Lefort's powerful essay on Solzhenitsyn, *Un homme en trop* (English translation to be published by

Urizen Books, New York, 1977).

14. The references from Claude Lefort are to his article, "Esquisse d'une genèse de l'idéologie dans les sociétés modernes," in *Textures* (Belgium) 74:8-9. A slightly altered version of this article appeared in the *Encyclopedia Universalis* under the title "L'ère de l'idéologie." On Lefort, to whom this interpretation is deeply indebted, see my "Introduction to Lefort," in *Telos* 23 (Winter 1974-75):1-20.

In the context of this argument, it is worth referring also to the former colleague of Lukács, Bela Fogarasi, whose article "Tasks of the Communist Press" was translated in *Radical America* 3, no. 3 (May-June 1969):68-75. Fogarasi points out that it is not so much in giving us false news or hiding the news from us that the capitalist press exercises its ideological and mystifying function—on the contrary, we have perhaps too much of it! What is missing is the context, the sense and meaning of the news.

15. Jean-Jacques Rousseau, *The Social Contract*, book 2, chap. 7. (The translation is mine.)

16. It is worth noting that the theoretically most interesting developments of a "New Left" theory are those of French thinkers from Deleuze and Guatari through Lyotard, Lefort, and Castoriadis. Common to all of them, emerging through structural linguistics, semiotics, and a certain "French Freud," is the critique of representational thought.

17. For the critique of Marx, see my volume *The Marxian Legacy* (London: Macmillan & Co.; New York: Urizen Books, 1977).

18. See note 16.

Notes to Chapter Six

1. "Working Papers of the Commission on the Year 2000" (Fourth Session held at the American Academy of Arts and Sciences in Boston, Mass., 24 October 1965), vol. 1, p. 146. Statement by Daniel Bell in response to Donald Schon who said that the Commission "set ourselves to say nothing that we are not then prepared to work on the social process for, to see how it can be used" (p. 145).

2. Karl Mannheim, *Man and Society in an Age of Reconstruction*, trans. Edward Shils (New York: Harcourt, Brace & World, 1940), pp. 110-111.

3. We may analogize the role of the futurologist to that of lawyers

whose purpose is to write and use inheritance laws and trusts to preserve the present class structure and present ruling consciousness into the future.

4. A number of the debates on planning, one aspect of futurology, centered at Columbia around the question raised by Max Horkheimer in his critique of Robert Lynd and John Dewey, the latter two seeing planning as a *sine qua non* for freedom.

5. Ossip K. Flechtheim, "Some Thoughts on the Future of Political Institutions," in Ossip K. Flechtheim, ed., *History and Futurology* (Meisenheim am Glan: Anton Hain Publishing House, 1966), p. 109.

6. Sir Basil Blackett, an important financier during the thirties, attempted to lead the British ruling class into planning. "First and foremost in the planning of national reconstruction came the necessity for a comprehensive insight and a firm grasp of the interrelationships between the various aspects of our political and economic and social life. The Cabinet Room at 10 Downing Street ought to have prominently emblazoned on its walls the Hegelian motto 'The Altogetherness of Everything.'" Quoted in John Strachey, *The Coming Struggle for Power* (New York: Modern Library, 1935), p. 245.

7. Quoted in Lucien Goldmann, *The Human Sciences and Philosophy*, trans. Hayden V. White and Robert Anchor (London: Cape Publishers, 1969), p. 147.

8. See John Dewey and James Tufts, *Ethics* (New York: Henry Holt & Co., 1908), pp. 470-535 passim.

9. Daniel Lerner and Harold D. Lasswell, eds., *The Policy Sciences* (Stanford, Calif.: Stanford University Press, 1951), p. 5.

10. Charles E. Rothwell, "Foreword," in *Policy Sciences*, p. ix.

11. See Robert Lynd, *Knowledge for What? The Place of Social Science in American Culture* (Princeton, N. J.: Princeton University Press, 1939).

12. One group, the Thomists, saw the question in a different light. They argued that it was a mistake to see man and nature as both infinitely pliable and manipulable, as most Marxists have seen man and nature. Believing in the natural law they sought an essence to him individually and as part of the group. It should be noted that this point of view has enormous and beneficial consequences because it starts with an inverted assumption. This position, shaped by natural rights thinkers and structuralists alike, states that there are inherent limits and boundaries and to breach them is to destroy the limits placed on actions against nature and the human other. Without those limits nature and man

would be so changed as to transform nature into hell and man's institutions into beastliness.

13. It should be noted that this sense of nonchoice, powerlessness, and unwillingness to "see" major social facts extends to state socialism as well. Mary McCarthy, by no means a radical writer, has pointed out, however, that noncapitalist economies will be able to encourage culture and art as well as local participation and initiative in a socialist setting because there is no intrinsic purpose such as profit. See Mary McCarthy, *The Seventeenth Degree* (New York: Harcourt Brace Jovanovich, 1974), pp. 184-185.

14. Horkheimer, *Eclipse of Reason* (New York: Oxford University Press, 1947), pp. 95-96.

15. Garrett Hardin, "Experts Discuss Future of the U.S.," in *Los Angeles Times,* 18 December 1974, p. 12.

16. Quoted in Quincy Wright, *A Study of War* (Chicago: University of Chicago Press, 1942), vol. 2, p. 1302.

17. Richard McKeon, *Thought, Action and Passion* (Chicago: Chicago University Press, 1954), p. 224.

18. Adolfa Sanchez Vazquez, *Art and Society—Essays in Marxist Aesthetics,* trans. Maro Riofrancos (New York: Monthly Review Press, 1974), p. 268.

19. McKeon, *Thought, Action and Passion,* p. 226.

20. Herman Kahn quoted in "Working Papers of the Commission on the Year 2000," vol. 2A, section A-1, p. 46.

21. Roger Garaudy, *The Alternative Future: A Vision of Christian Marxism,* trans. Leonard Mayhew (New York: Simon & Schuster, 1974), p. 98.

22. Paul Goodman, *Speaking and Language: Defence of Poetry* (New York: Random House, 1971), p. 202.

23. Gunther S. Stent, *The Coming of the Golden Age: A View of the End of Progress* (Garden City, N. Y.: Natural History Press, 1969), p. 105.

24. Garaudy, *Alternative Future,* p. 99.

25. Sanchez Vazquez, *Art and Society,* pp. 270 and 272-273.

26. Ibid., p. 274.

27. See Dewey and Tufts, *Ethics,* chap. 20.